Harvard Business Review

ON

MANAGING EXTERNAL RISK

THE HARVARD BUSINESS REVIEW PAPERBACK SERIES

The series is designed to bring today's managers and professionals the fundamental information they need to stay competitive in a fast-moving world. From the preeminent thinkers whose work has defined an entire field to the rising stars who will redefine the way we think about business, here are the leading minds and landmark ideas that have established the *Harvard Business Review* as required reading for ambitious businesspeople in organizations around the globe.

Other books in the series:

Other books in the series (continued):

Harvard Business Review on Culture and Change
Harvard Business Review on Customer Relationship Management
Harvard Business Review on Decision Making
Harvard Business Review on Developing Leaders
Harvard Business Review on Doing Business in China
Harvard Business Review on Effective Communication
Harvard Business Review on Entrepreneurship
Harvard Business Review on Finding and Keeping the Best People
Harvard Business Review on Green Business Strategy
Harvard Business Review on the High-Performance Organization
Harvard Business Review on Innovation
Harvard Business Review on the Innovative Enterprise
Harvard Business Review on Knowledge Management
Harvard Business Review on Leadership
Harvard Business Review on Leadership at the Top
Harvard Business Review on Leadership in a Changed World
Harvard Business Review on Leading in Turbulent Times
Harvard Business Review on Leading Through Change
Harvard Business Review on Making Smarter Decisions
Harvard Business Review on Managing Diversity
Harvard Business Review on Managing Health Care
Harvard Business Review on Managing High-Tech Industries
Harvard Business Review on Managing People
Harvard Business Review on Managing Projects
Harvard Business Review on Managing Through a Downturn
Harvard Business Review on Managing Uncertainty
Harvard Business Review on Managing the Value Chain
Harvard Business Review on Managing Your Career
Harvard Business Review on Managing Yourself

Other books in the series (continued):

Harvard Business Review

ON

MANAGING EXTERNAL RISK

ISBN: 978-1-4221-3844-1

Library-of-Congress cataloging information available

Contents

The New Arsenal
of Risk Management

KEVIN BUEHLER, ANDREW FREEMAN,
AND RON HULME

Executive Summary

THE GLOBAL BANKING SYSTEM is facing a
severe liquidity crisis: In the first half of 2008,
major financial institutions wrote off nearly $400
billion, causing banks around the world to initiate
emergency measures. Similar crises have occurred
within recent memory: Think of S&Ls, the dot-com
bust, and Enron. Risk is, quite simply, a fact of corporate life—but because risk-management research
has increasingly emphasized mathematical modeling, managers may find it incomprehensible and
thus shy away from powerful tools and markets for
creating value.

Buehler, Freeman, and Hulme, all with
McKinsey, describe the evolution of risk management since the 1970s, show how new markets

have changed the landscape in both financial services and the energy sector, and explain what it takes to compete in the current environment. To demonstrate how significant a factor risk can be when incorporated into strategy and organization, they take the case of Goldman Sachs—which, despite its reliance on highly volatile trading revenues, has so far avoided the big write-offs that have afflicted its leading competitors. The authors believe that this is because Goldman takes the antithesis of the typical corporate approach—its culture embraces rather than avoids risk. And, they say, Goldman very efficiently employs all four of the following factors: quantitative professionals, strong oversight, partnership investment, and a clear statement of business principles, with emphasis on preserving the company's reputation.

Staying on the sidelines of risk management may have shielded some companies from crisis, but it has also prevented them from growing as quickly as they might have. In their companion article, "Owning the Right Risks," the authors outline a process that will enable executives in any company to incorporate risk into their strategic decision making.

Dɪꜱᴄᴜꜱꜱɪᴏɴꜱ ᴏꜰ ʀɪꜱᴋ usually come to the forefront in times of crisis but then recede as normalcy returns. As we write, the global banking system is facing a major credit and liquidity crisis. Losses from subprime mortgages, structured investment vehicles, and "covenant lite" loans are creating a credit crunch that may in turn trigger a global slowdown. In the past year major financial institutions have written off nearly $400 billion, and central banks around the world have initiated emergency measures to restore liquidity. Several other crises have occurred within memory: the U.S. savings-and-loan collapse in the 1980s and 1990s, Black Monday in 1987, the Russian debt default and the related dive of Long-Term Capital Management in 1998, the dot-com bust of 2000, and the Enron-led merchant-power collapse of 2001.

The resounding message is that risk is always with us. Executives need to wake up to that fact. Unfortunately, a growing emphasis on mathematical modeling has rendered much of the risk-management debate and research incomprehensible to those outside the finance function and the financial services industry. As a result, many corporate managers have shied away from the powerful risk-management tools and markets created over the past three decades—and thus have forgone considerable opportunities to create value.

Our aim here is to help managers understand both the advantages and the limitations of the markets and tools that are implicated in the credit and liquidity crisis. We will describe the evolution of risk management in recent decades, show how new markets have changed the landscape in both financial services and the energy sector, and explain what it takes to compete in the current environment. These analyses will help readers make sense of the crisis and will illustrate just how powerful a lens risk can be when applied to corporate strategy and organization. In the companion article published in this issue, we describe a process whereby executives in all companies can incorporate risk into their strategic decision making.

The Idea That Changed the World

For the first 70 years of the twentieth century, corporate risk management was largely about buying insurance. Risk management in the financial sector was also rudimentary: Bank regulators lacked tools for measuring risk in the system, so constructive intervention was difficult. Banks themselves had no way to control the interest-rate risk in their loan portfolios or to quantify and manage credit risk—in part because few alternatives to insurance existed. To be sure, some futures and options contracts were written and sold, but reliable tools for pricing them were rare, and the markets for these securities were thin and characterized by wide bid-ask spreads.

The low level of interest in risk management was also to some extent a product of prevailing thought in finance, originating with Franco Modigliani and Merton Miller's "indifference theory," which argued that a company's value was not (in most cases) affected by capital structure or hedging, and the capital asset pricing model (CAPM), developed by William Sharpe and others, which argued that risk should be managed primarily through portfolio diversification by investors. (For a summary of the main theories relating to the field, see the exhibit "The Evolution of Risk Management.")

All this began to change in 1973, with the publication of the options-pricing model developed by Fischer Black and Myron Scholes and expanded on by Robert C. Merton. The new model enabled more-effective pricing and mitigation of risk. It could calculate the value of an option to buy a security as long as the user could supply five pieces of data: the risk-free rate of return (usually defined as the return on a three-month U.S. Treasury bill), the price at which the security would be purchased

The Evolution of Risk Management

This timeline describes milestones in the development of risk management and their relevance today.

1952: Mean variance (aka modern portfolio theory)
Harry Markowitz

Essence: Investors can analyze risk as well as their expected return

Relevance: Provides the basis for portfolio choices to achieve the optimal level of risk for a given return

Late 1950s, early 1960s: State preference theory
Kenneth Arrow, Gérard Debreu

Essence: An efficient allocation of resources and risks requires a "complete" set of securities that permits agents to hedge all risks

Relevance: Underpins derivatives and shows that the ultimate role of securities markets is to efficiently allocate risk across society

1958: "Indifference theory"
Franco Modigliani, Merton Miller

Essence: In a perfect market (no taxes, bankruptcy costs, or asymmetric information), the value of a company is independent of its capital structure

Relevance: Doesn't hold true in the real world, suggesting the need for efficient capital structure and risk mitigation through hedging

1960s: Capital asset pricing model (CAPM)
William Sharpe et al.

Essence: Markets compensate investors for accepting *systematic*—or market—risk, but do not discount for *idiosyncratic* risk, which is specific to an individual asset and can be eliminated through diversification

Relevance: Affects decisions about hedging—which should be left to investors—and about whether or not to mitigate specific risks

1973: Options-pricing model
Fischer Black, Myron Scholes, Robert C. Merton

Essence: The volatility of a security is a key factor in options prices

Relevance: Allows major new risk transfer, while the related field of real options means companies can put a value on waiting

1976: Arbitrage pricing theory
Stephen Ross

Essence: The price of a security is driven by a number of factors, which are either macroeconomic or market indices

Relevance: Permits segmentation of CAPM systematic risk into factors or components. If prices diverge from expected returns, investors can use arbitrage to bring them back into line

1977: Underinvestment problem
Stewart Myers, Clifford Smith, René M. Stulz

Essence: Stockholders refuse to invest in low-risk/low-return assets to avoid shifting wealth from themselves to debt holders (mirror image of the asset substitution problem)

Relevance: Suggests there is potential shareholder value in better risk management through better investment decisions

1979: Binomial option pricing model
John Cox, Stephen Ross, Mark Rubinstein

Essence: Taking into account variations over time in the price of the underlying financial instrument leads to more-accurate pricing of some options

Relevance: Allows much deeper markets for long-dated options and options on securities paying dividends

1993: A framework for risk management including hedging
Kenneth Froot, David Scharfstein, Jeremy Stein

Essence: The goal of risk management is to ensure that a company has cash available for value-enhancing investments

Relevance: Theoretically supports managers trying to manage risk as a strategic set of choices

(usually given), the current price at which the security was traded (to be observed in the market), the remaining time during which the option could be exercised (given), and the security's price volatility (which could be estimated from historical data and is now more commonly inferred from the prices of options themselves if they are traded). The equations in the model assume that the underlying security's price mimics the random way in which air molecules move in space, familiar to engineers as Brownian motion.

The core idea addressed by Black-Scholes was optionality: Embedded in all instruments, capital structures, and business portfolios are options that can expire, be exercised, or be sold. In many cases an option is both obvious and bounded—as is, for example, an option to buy General Electric stock at a given price for a given period. Other options are subtler. In their 1973 paper Black and Scholes pointed out that the holders of equity in a company with debt in its capital structure have an option to buy back the firm from the debt holders at a strike price equal to the company's debt. Similarly, the emerging field of real options identified those implicit in a company's operations—for example, the option to cancel or defer a project based on information from a pilot. The theory of real options put a value on managerial flexibility—something overlooked in straightforward NPV calculations, which assume an all-or-nothing attitude toward projects.

The new model could hardly have come at a more propitious time, coinciding as it did with the spread of the handheld electronic calculator. Texas Instruments marketed an early version to financial professionals with the tagline "Now you can find the Black-Scholes value using our calculator." The calculator's rapid acceptance by options traders fueled the growth in derivatives markets and the broad development of standard pricing models. Other technological advances quickly followed: In 1975 the first personal computers were launched. In 1979 Dan Bricklin and Bob Frankston released VisiCalc, the first spreadsheet designed to work on a personal computer, giving managers a simple tool with which to run what-if scenarios. The financial sector rapidly developed new instruments for managing different types of risk and began trading them on exchanges—notably the Chicago Board Options Exchange—and in over-the-counter derivatives markets.

By the 1980s, with calculating muscle inexorably increasing on the trading desk, it had become far easier to identify, price, and trade different kinds of options. Among the most influential machines were workstations developed by Sun Microsystems and Digital Equipment and the Bloomberg Terminal, which revolutionized price calculation in derivatives and fixed-income markets respectively. Crystal Ball and other firms developed software that allowed traders to run Monte Carlo simulations in a matter of minutes on laptops, rather than overnight on mainframe computers. By the beginning of the 1990s it was possible to buy contracts that covered a wide variety of risks using derivatives of various kinds— options, futures, and swaps, often in combination. Derivatives markets began with currencies, equities, and interest rates and quickly expanded to include energy, metals, and other commodities. In a second wave of innovation, instruments emerged that allowed the hedging or transfer of credit risk, at that time the major remaining category of financial risk and a subject of concern among bank regulators. By the end of the decade derivatives markets were exploding; the notional value of the securities involved rose from $72 trillion in 1998 to $370 trillion in 2006. By the end of 2007 the total had reached almost $600 trillion. The market was so sophisticated that "synthetic CDOs"—derivatives of derivatives of derivatives—soon appeared and in fact were the fastest-growing sector of the multitrillion-dollar market for collateralized debt obligations until the credit crunch began in late 2007.

But optionality goes well beyond financial services. It implies that a company's equity is a basket option in which its various risks are pooled: Each shareholder is exposed to a tiny fraction of the risk to which the company is subject. A simple but useful way to think about a company's balance sheet, therefore, is to see its equity as a cushion against the risk of performing badly. The risk that its market value will go down is borne by the shareholders. No such cushion is provided by debt, on which the interest must be paid no matter how the company performs.

Two conclusions follow: First, any company has an appropriate debt-to-equity ratio, geared to the probability that it will suffer losses. Too large a cushion—more equity capital than is required—means that the company is using capital inefficiently. (If it has issued shares to raise "excess" equity capital, profits will have to increase if it is to maintain the previous rate of return.) Too small a cushion means the company is not just courting default or financial distress but also may be ignoring or deferring growth opportunities in response to smaller-than-expected operating cash flows.

Second, because the optimal debt level is determined by a company's key market, financial, and operating risks, it is directly affected by actions that mitigate those risks. Managers can therefore add value by separately and more cheaply hedging some of the risks ordinarily managed by the equity cushion. As Robert Merton pointed out in "You Have More Capital than You Think" (HBR November 2005), some companies are better than others at managing particular risks. If risks can be priced and traded, it makes sense for companies to try to lay off the categories of risk in which they have no comparative advantage. This approach allows them to reserve their (expensive) equity capital for risks that would cost more to transfer than to manage directly.

The work of Merton and other leading academics validated the growing field of risk management and counterbalanced indifference theory. Let's now look at how risk management has developed in the financial sector.

The Revolution in Financial Services

Many important innovations in risk management originated in the banking and securities industries. The reasons are obvious but worth stating. First, financial institutions are in effect risk-intermediation businesses; as the most sophisticated of them came to realize, the ability to describe, price, and manage risk should be among their core competencies. Second, these industries are rich in data, and thus a natural locus for efforts to quantify risk using new technologies. Third, and perhaps most important, they are typically highly leveraged and are monitored by regulators who, concerned about the potential impact of failures, pushed for improved risk management. That concern went back at least to 1974, when Herstatt, a German bank, failed and a lot of international banks were badly hurt because of the time lag involved in cross-border settlements. Foreign-exchange transactions executed in Germany had not yet cleared in New York when the bank was declared insolvent, creating enormous exposures.

In the following decades banks faced several comparable crises involving interest-rate and credit risk, among them the infamous S&L collapse. In the early 1990s an economic slowdown and listless real estate markets caused an unexpected surge in defaults among commercial banks' borrowers. A number of leading financial institutions were in grave danger of going bust; one survived in significant part owing to an enormous investment by a private individual. Bank of New England, among others, did actually go under.

At bottom, poor risk management was to blame. Banks had only a limited understanding of the credit risks in their loan portfolios; their assets and liabilities were typically mismatched; and they retained loss-making exposures on their balance sheets. Even in the early 1990s most commercial banks lacked now commonplace tools such as VaR (value at risk), credit risk portfolio models, and RAROC (risk-adjusted return on capital).

In contrast, securities firms and investment banks had become quite sophisticated in their use of risk-management tools. They recognized that much of traditional commercial banking could emulate the trading of shares and bonds. Bank loans could be marked to market (that is, priced as if they must be sold immediately, even though they might not mature for years to come), turned into securities, and traded. Loan portfolios could be packaged in tranches. Interest-rate risk could be separated from credit risk. And so on. Because securities firms and investment banks were skilled at packaging and trading risks, and commercial banks were skilled at originating credit, a wave of mergers began; eventually distinctions between the two kinds of organizations blurred and regulatory barriers diminished.

Beginning in the mid-1980s the financial sector became a gigantic risk clearinghouse, as highly liquid markets for the transfer of all sorts of risk evolved. Because companies could transfer risk that had previously been cushioned by equity, more equity was available to generate new business where they had a natural competitive advantage. Commercial banks, for example, could lay off interest-rate risk and seek out additional depositors and creditors. More recently they have laid off credit risk as well, further increasing their ability to grow. As of this writing, of course, liquidity in the securitization and credit-transfer markets has dried up, dramatically diminishing the origination of credit. It remains to be seen how events will unfold; but even if a backlash occurs against some complex structured instruments, financial innovators are extremely unlikely to stop repackaging and trading risks.

Let's look now at the markets and institutions most deeply involved in both the growth of risk transfer and the current risk-management crisis.

MORTGAGES

The mortgage market perhaps best illustrates how risk instruments can transform the scope and nature of a business and also what the limitations are of relying too heavily on markets for risk management. Traditionally, banks held their mortgages in a single portfolio. In the early 1980s, especially in the United States, they started to securitize these portfolios: They pooled their mortgages, divided the pools into tranches, and sold them to third-party investors—other banks, pension funds, or insurance companies. In this way the risks of mortgage default were taken off the books of the original banks, which went on to make further mortgage loans (and to collect the associated fees), which were also pooled. This growth in business led to unprecedented profitability in the banking sector. But by early 2007 it was clear that both the underwriting and the rating of mortgages had become far too lax, so when subprime default rates rose, a major financial crisis ensued. Its ramifications are still spreading. The higher default rates rapidly depressed the prices of mortgage securitizations, first of the lower-rated tranches and then of the higher-rated ones. Some global banks, though they were not direct U.S. mortgage lenders, held portfolios of highly rated mortgage-backed securities or CDOs of mortgage-backed securities. As the ratings of those securities dropped, the banks' equity cushions thinned; they had to write off billions of dollars in asset values, seek out huge infusions of capital, and sharply reduce lending. The resulting credit crunch has changed the policy landscape, creating pressure for interest-rate cuts and giving rise to special lending facilities for liquidity-starved financial institutions. But risk can still be sliced and diced into discrete elements. The lesson here is not that the banks were wrong to take advantage of the markets but that even the largest and most liquid derivatives markets depend on the quality of the underlying assets. Transferring risk does not mean eliminating risk.

WHOLESALE CREDIT

Financial innovation has influenced corporate credit as well, triggering a boom in commercial lending. Commercial banks can now refine their portfolios to retain only those risk categories in which they have a comparative advantage—perhaps an information advantage in the middle market, where customers are more idiosyncratic. They can modify exposure with credit-default swaps— derivative instruments that protect against a given company's financial distress. They can also use index derivative products to raise or lower their overall exposure to credit as an asset class if they believe that credit is too cheap or too expensive. Thus they can lend more to a particular customer without increasing their overall exposure to that customer's sector or increase their exposure to a sector without necessarily having to make fresh loans. Once again, transferring risk in these ways can free up capital for growth, enabling banks to offer more and more credit.

The main buyers of transferred risk have been pension and hedge funds, insurers, and others seeking the diversification provided by assets whose returns aren't directly correlated to stock and bond markets. But the liquidity of wholesale credit markets, like that of mortgages, cannot be taken for granted. The mortgage crisis has made investors less willing to participate in the securitization and credit-transfer markets. What's more, the ability to estimate credit-risk exposure has not kept pace with the growth in credit-risk instruments; during 2007 it became evident that banks were struggling to cope with the complexity of their portfolios. Although companies can separate out and trade individual risks, counterparty credit risk is often created as a result, and this needs to be monitored and managed. If a company has a credit exposure to an institution with which it has laid off some other risk, it still may be indirectly exposed to that underlying risk.

HEDGE FUNDS AND PRIVATE EQUITY

The creation and growth of risk-transfer markets enabled fundamental changes in the investment management industry. Professional investors took advantage of their newfound ability to transfer different kinds of risk by creating investment vehicles not subject to some of the regulations on traditional funds (typically, those open to the public). Hedge funds are one such vehicle; they have rapidly evolved to allow investors to be extremely precise about their exposure across different asset classes, time horizons, and so on. In addition, as investors in CDOs and other asset-backed securities, they can help absorb credit risk from the banking system. Hedge funds are controversial: Do they introduce new risks into financial markets by using leverage to boost their returns? Do they really control the risks they run, or are they vulnerable to liquidity shocks and gaming by their competitors? These questions arose after Long-Term Capital Management's failure and again in 2006, when in a single week Amaranth Advisors, a commodity hedge fund, lost $6 billion of its $9 billion of assets under management by betting on natural-gas futures. More-recent hedge-fund failures have occurred, most publicly at Bear Stearns. Nevertheless, the sector has continued its strong growth, even during the market ructions of 2007–2008.

Private equity has been equally dynamic: Aggressive, capital-rich firms now stalk the world's markets looking to profit from taking listed companies into private ownership. Although private equity is not often described in terms of risk management (most PE firms stress their financial and governance skills), it can be regarded as applying cutting-edge risk-management techniques. PE deals have often relied on complex structured finance tools to lower capital costs through debt and hedging. It remains unclear how much private equity will suffer from the reduced liquidity of late 2007, but strong growth continues in this sector as well.

Risk as Culture: The Case of Goldman Sachs

As the markets for risk have evolved, it has become clear that a company's success is closely linked to the role risk plays in its culture. In the financial sector there is no better model than Goldman Sachs, arguably the world's leading investment banking, securities, and investment management firm. Today Goldman is essentially in the business of managing risk: Trading and principal investments account for 68% of its net revenues, whereas only 17% come from the traditional investment-banking and advisory business for which it was once best known.

Yet despite its reliance on highly volatile trading revenues (and the company's trading revenues are more volatile than any of its peers'), Goldman has so far avoided the large losses that have afflicted its leading competitors. In our view, this is because the firm's culture embraces rather than avoids risk—the antithesis of the typical corporate approach. Goldman makes money by being willing to risk losing it. When securities markets become more volatile, options rise in value; naturally, the value of experienced risk management rises also. Goldman ensures that its managers are familiar and comfortable with risk, can debate it freely without fear of sanctions, and are willing to make decisions quickly when necessary. The company's aggressive hedging in 2007 in markets related to subprime mortgages was a striking example of this. Goldman was both skillful and lucky. It was skillful in sensing that trouble was brewing and deciding to move quickly to reposition itself. It was lucky in getting both the decision and the timing correct.

Creating a culture so contrary to people's instincts and fears isn't easy. In our view, Goldman's success stems from four factors. None is unique to the company, but Goldman very effectively employs all four.

QUANTITATIVE PROFESSIONALS

Beginning in the early 1980s, Goldman recruited experts in mathematical modeling, who came to be called quants. Perhaps the most notable hire was Fischer Black,

brought over from MIT in 1984 by Robert Rubin, who
was then a general partner. Black led the firm's Quantitative Strategies group, working on, among other things,
modern portfolio management and modeling interest-
rate movements in order to value fixed-income options.
Goldman also hired Emanuel Derman, a PhD in theoretical physics and one of Black's successors as head of
Quantitative Strategies; and Bob Litterman, a PhD in
economics and a codeveloper of the Black-Litterman
global asset allocation model. People like these provided
the quantitative and intellectual rigor needed to support
Goldman's complex trading and derivatives businesses.

STRONG OVERSIGHT

In 1994, when an unexpected rise in global interest rates
caused severe losses on many bond-trading desks, Goldman's large proprietary positions led to a substantial
decline in profitability and a crisis in morale. In
response, Jon Corzine, who had just assumed leadership
of the company, restructured Goldman's risk-control
systems, establishing the Firmwide Risk Committee to
oversee market and credit risk worldwide. The committee, which meets weekly, aims to ensure that certain risk-
return standards are applied consistently across the firm.
Daily risk reports detail the firm's exposure with, for
example, summary sheets showing the potential impact
of changes in various macro risk factors and stress tests
showing potential losses under a variety of scenarios,
such as a widening of credit spreads, as happened in the
autumn of 1998. Some Goldman executives claim they
can fairly accurately estimate the firm's daily P&L just by
looking at the risk reports and knowing the market's

movements that day. Other forms of risk are taken equally seriously: Operational and reputational risks are addressed by the Business Practices Committee, loan and underwriting risks are addressed by the Capital and Commitments committees, and liquidity risk is managed by the Finance Committee.

PARTNERSHIP HERITAGE

From its earliest days in 1869 to its IPO in 1999, Goldman was funded largely by its own partners. But while Lazard Frères and other private firms distributed more than 80% of their earnings each year, Goldman's partners usually left as much as 80% of their after-tax earnings in the firm, withdrawing substantial amounts of capital only at retirement. The partners were careful stewards of the firm's capital because it was their own. Goldman's most senior executives continue this heritage, and the fact that employees still own a significant portion of equity helps reinforce the partnership culture.

BUSINESS PRINCIPLES

Finally, Goldman's values reinforce many of these risk-management lessons. The company's reputation is prized most of all. New hires are taught that although no single individual can make the firm successful, anyone can harm its reputation. They are encouraged to solicit independent views from risk, compliance, legal, and other powerful control functions when potentially controversial choices arise. The fastest way to get fired at Goldman is not to lose money but to make a unilateral decision that endangers the reputation of the firm.

The Revolution in Energy

As the success of markets for transferring financial risk
became evident, companies in other sectors began to
consider creating similar mechanisms. Commodity businesses that already had highly liquid spot markets were
obvious candidates. The energy sector clearly had an
enormous latent demand for risk transfer: Oil and gas
producers would benefit hugely if they could lay off price
risk in order to facilitate debt financing and concentrate
on exploration and extraction. Oil refineries and other
energy processors face even greater margin volatility
from both crude oil and refined products. Deregulated
power generators, which produce electricity—a commodity that must be sold as it is made, forcing prices up
or down whenever it is under- or overproduced—face the
greatest volatility of all. Moreover, all these companies
must commit very large investments (several billion dollars for a single refinery, oil platform, or power plant)
over 30 to 50 years, with all the industry ups and downs
and technological advances that period may encompass.

Thus the rapid growth of energy futures markets like
the NYMEX and ICE, along with over-the-counter derivatives markets, is unsurprising. In the 1990s major oil
companies such as BP; electric utilities such as Duke
Energy, Sempra, and RWE; and natural-gas companies
such as Dynegy, El Paso, and Williams invested heavily
to build large commodity-trading and risk-intermediation businesses. The most notable player, of course,
was Enron, which had more than 1,000 energy traders
and—even after post-scandal income restatements—
more than $2 billion in annual trading profits. Enron also
provided risk-management services and structured
finance to oil and gas producers and service companies.

Immediately prior to the company's collapse, Enron Online was regularly settling transactions in excess of $4 billion a day.

Following Enron's bankruptcy, energy commodity markets briefly dried up. Several other trading-oriented companies, including Dynegy, El Paso, Reliant, and Mirant, suffered big losses; some narrowly avoided their own bankruptcies. Credit concerns and the loss of liquidity formerly provided by Enron greatly reduced potential trading profits. Wanting to distance themselves from trading and derivatives, many industrial participants shut down their trading floors.

But retrenchment was short-lived, because the fundamental need for financing and volatility reduction persisted. Investment banks (and, later, hedge funds) quickly stepped in, hiring the talent formerly employed by Enron and other industrial players. Over the past two years two leading investment banks alone have reported more than $3 billion in profits from energy and commodity trading and risk management. Merrill Lynch, UBS, Royal Bank of Scotland, and Lehman each acquired trading operations from industry players. By the end of 2007 liquidity was approaching the levels of 2001.

Despite the availability of these liquid risk-transfer markets, however, only a few energy companies—those with an insatiable need for risk capital—have fully embraced strategic risk management. The scandals and stigma associated with complex derivatives are no doubt partly to blame, but the unprecedented surge in earnings in virtually all segments of the industry is probably more so. From 1999 to 2005 the 64 companies in Standard & Poor's energy and utilities sectors saw annual operating cash flows increase from $95 billion to $245 billion.

The companies that *have* embraced strategic risk management are among the most successful. The start-up Flores & Rucks (later Ocean Energy and now merged into Devon Energy) grew into a leading independent producer using volumetric production payments—loans secured by underlying oil and gas assets—and other structured finance vehicles. Chesapeake Energy has become an industry leader in U.S. exploration and production with a business model based on fully hedging its natural-gas price exposure. Refiners such as Valero, Tosco, and Premcor have used hedging strategies to support dramatic acquisition-based growth. Suncor, a pioneer in Canadian oil sands, used hedging to sustain its capital-intensive program through industry down cycles. Anadarko used bridge financing and hedging to enable two largely debt-funded acquisitions whose total cost exceeded its own market capitalization.

As these companies demonstrate, transferring risk can confer enormous strategic benefits. Because they are focusing their human and financial capital where they enjoy a comparative advantage, they can create more value than competitors that waste equity capital on risks that others will quite willingly assume.

OVER THE PAST THREE decades all kinds of tools and techniques for risk management have emerged. They have revolutionized financial services and energy, creating gigantic markets for the transfer of specific kinds of risk and generating billions of dollars in profit. They have freed up huge amounts of equity capital, enabling those industries to grow much faster than other sectors; by some estimates, the contribution of the finance sector alone to U.S. GDP has doubled in the past

30 years, from around 4% to 8%—at a time when the economy overall grew from roughly $1.6 trillion to more than $14 trillion.

Of course, risk-management tools carry dangers, as the crises in both finance and energy demonstrate. But it would be a big mistake for mainstream corporate executives to conclude that trying to manage risk is too dangerous. Staying on the sidelines may have shielded some companies from crisis, but it has also prevented them from growing as quickly as they might have. And continuing to avoid the game, now that we're coming to understand the limitations of risk-management markets and instruments, will only compound the mistake. The time has come to take stock of what we know and to learn how and when these incredibly powerful instruments should be used in "ordinary" corporations. That is what we address in "Owning the Right Risks."

Originally published in September 2008
Reprint R0809G

A Letter to the Chief Executive

JOSEPH FULLER

Executive Summary

BEYOND THE RECENT ACCOUNTING scandals, something is wrong with the way most companies are managed today. That's the message of this fictional letter from a board member to a CEO, written by Joseph Fuller, CEO of strategy consulting firm the Monitor Group.

The letter highlights the challenges and complexities of running a business in today's uncertain environment. And while it avoids the facile bashing of U.S. executives so common these days, the missive nonetheless casts a harsh light on the flaws that have recently been exposed in the American management model.

The letter addresses a single CEO and company, yet it is intended to speak to executives and boards everywhere:

"It wasn't the recession that caused us to make three acquisitions in two years at very, very high prices; the need to fuel [unreasonable] growth did. Nor was it the recession that caused us to expand our capacity in anticipation of gaining market share; rather, it was our own overly optimistic sales forecasts that led us to that decision. Where did those forecasts originate? From line managers trying to fulfill profit goals that we created after meeting with the analysts.

"The root cause of many of the problems that became apparent in the last 24 months lies not with the economy, not with September 11, and not with the dot-com bubble. Rather, it lies with that willingness to be led by outside forces— indeed, our own lack of conviction about setting a course."

Restoring sound, strategic decision making— thinking that looks beyond tomorrow's analyst reports—will go a long way toward keeping those outside forces at bay, according to Fuller.

D EAR CEO,

I've been reflecting on the recent board meeting. We were all encouraged by the third-quarter revenue numbers and the improving forecast for the year. The stabilization of our gross margin, despite the price cuts, speaks well of your latest cost reduction initiatives. On the whole, I think we can safely assume we've weathered the current storm. However, while we can all be grateful for the recent signs of an upturn in our performance, I suspect the next year or two will hold many challenges.

Indeed, the stabilization of our situation offers only a brief reprieve, if any at all. Like many companies these days, we have a workforce that remains fragile after surviving rounds of layoffs. We operate in an industry that still has decidedly too much capacity. And we are embroiled in a market share battle that shows no signs of abating. I'm not sure if anyone really knows which of our competitors started the price war—for all I know, we did—but we've only just begun to see the effects on margins and market share. Furthermore, some of our competitors' recent earnings restatements and their use of "creative" accounting will surely bring more scrutiny to our company in the months ahead. In short, you'll have your hands full indefinitely.

That is precisely why I'm writing to share some thoughts on a less obvious, but nonetheless critical, issue: your role as the leader of the company during this time of uncertainty. I know I risk sounding like every pundit in America when I raise these issues, but I want to talk to you openly about your role and responsibilities in the future. I think my long service on the board and those years we spent working together on the industry council have earned me that right. Or perhaps, merely your indulgence.

I will spare you a sermon on the need for integrity in our financial reporting. I must admit, however, that even by the jaded standards of someone who has served as a director of public companies for more than 15 years, I'm shocked by what we've witnessed in the last several years. As the chair of the Audit Committee, I remain

satisfied both with the accuracy of our financial reporting and the performance of our auditors. Similarly, I'm
not concerned about the level of your compensation or
dealing in our stock. Nonetheless, we must guard against
even the appearance of rapaciousness or self-dealing, lest
we invite intense scrutiny from the business press, the
union, and institutional investors.

This risk is just one way in which the current circumstances have thrust you into a position where your
actions will have a disproportionate impact on the company's prospects. As the famous World War II admiral
Bull Halsey once said, "There are no great men, only
great challenges that ordinary men are forced by circumstances to meet." I think the next couple of years will
offer those "great challenges" and will require all your
skill to meet them. Another observation: Whether you
like it or not, your career is apt to be judged by your
performance over that period.

As you know, I've watched this industry closely for
many years—seven of them as a CEO myself—and this
isn't the first downturn I've seen. As I've thought about it,
though, I've come to reject most of the analogies between
this and previous recessions as flawed. In my view, the
most important feature of this recession is what happened
in the years preceding it. It was during that time that we
fell victim both to our hubris and to the pressures to per-
form up to Wall Street's expectations instead of our own.

In retrospect, it is now clear that because of our desire
to "meet or beat the street," we made a number of strategic choices and instigated a series of changes to the
underlying management system that caused us to fall
harder and faster than necessary. For example, you and

the CFO consistently told the market that we could grow profits at a 15% compound annual rate, even though our core businesses were struggling to hit 4% top-line growth and we were close to exhausting our supply of sensible cost reduction options. Sure, the consultants told us it was possible. And yes, the rest of the board and I got caught up in the rhetoric and went along. But look where that left us when the downturn hit.

After all, it wasn't the recession that caused us to make three acquisitions in two years at very, very high prices (ah, the benefit of hindsight!); the need to fuel that growth did. Nor was it the recession that caused us to expand our capacity in anticipation of gaining market share; rather, it was our own overly optimistic sales forecasts that led us to that decision. Where did those forecasts originate? From line managers trying to fulfill profit goals that we created after meeting with the analysts. Because we bought into the analysts' logic instead of asserting our own, we ended up with unrealistic goals and similarly unrealistic plans to meet them.

We didn't just add marginal plant and equipment, but marginal people as well, right across the workforce. The tight labor market scared us and we overreacted. We had the hiring spigot turned on all the way almost until the day we pulled the plug. No wonder the Internet chat rooms are full of angry comments. We changed the story we were telling employees practically in midsentence. It wasn't the tight labor market, though, that caused us to increase executive compensation and, especially, to award options to everyone at the vice-president level and above. The Compensation Committee did that with the input and encouragement of management. (Again, as a former member of that committee, I have to shoulder some of the blame here.) The liberal granting of options helped create a generation of executives who now think they're entitled to become millionaires.

I'm not saying these decisions and others were necessarily all that wrongheaded at the time. As I reflect on it, however, one thing does stand out. I think we were guilty of focusing more on what others expected of us than on what we knew was the real potential of the company and the real opportunities in our industry. In the last few years, we've defined our strategy more and more in terms of outcomes—How do we grow revenue at this rate, or EPS at that rate?—and less and less around the substantive decisions that actually drive those outcomes—How do we gain leadership in this market, or should we invest in that technology? Driven by the need to meet stretch financial goals, we've invested in plants making products that are only marginally profitable. We've ventured into new markets without asking whether we'll be able to wrest share from rivals who intend to defend their turf as fiercely as we defend ours. In short, we took new initiatives simply because they gave us some hope of making our numbers, not because we were confident that the business logic was sound.

Despite what the headlines say, I think the root cause of many of the problems that became apparent in the last 24 months lies not with the economy, not with September 11, and not with the dot-com bubble. Rather, it lies with that willingness to be led by outside forces— indeed, our own lack of conviction about setting a course. Now that things are settling down a bit, I think you need to take a deep breath and think about how to use this *annus horribilis* as an opportunity to break some bad habits. Specifically, I think you should use it to alter the fundamental nature of the conversations you've been having with some of your key constituencies: Wall Street, the board, the senior executive team, and the rank-and-file workforce. Since last year's performance eliminated any chance of fulfilling the expectations we helped create in each of these constituencies, let's reboot and set expectations that are based on reality.

L ET S START WITH Wall Street. During my 15 years on your board, I've watched as the agenda of the board meetings has become more and more focused on the analysts, their expectations, whether we'll meet them, et cetera, et cetera. Until recently, we talked about how to manage these expectations. Even though the SEC has put the kibosh on all the private, in-depth briefings and whispered conversations with analysts, we're still spending too much time figuring out whether and where we'll fall in their expected range. In my view, that's putting the cart before the horse. Too often, last year's "strategic initiatives" have been scrapped in the interest of this quarter's earnings. Investments and acquisitions we had celebrated as major growth vehicles have been pared back, sold, or written off—in response to skepticism from analysts or the rating agencies as much as out of managerial conviction.

What bothers me is that we seem to have lost control of the situation. We spend more time talking about what the analysts think we should earn than we do discussing what the company is capable of earning. I realize that we have a credenza full of bankers' reports telling us that "high performance" companies grow their earnings at 15% annually. I just haven't seen the corresponding study showing how you do that in a market that is growing in the single digits, with a company that has gone through multiple waves of cost reduction and asset rationalization.

Once upon a time, analysts studied companies in order to understand their potential, describe the case for investing to their clients, and make recommendations. Many of them developed a deep understanding of how particular companies had positioned themselves, how the fundamental economics of an industry worked, and what company-specific risks various players faced. Admittedly, the world and our business have gotten more complicated during my tenure on the board, but it seems to me that many of our current analysts don't have that type of understanding. When news is grim, they always seem shocked, scurrying to rewrite their estimates and relegating companies that surprise them to the "penalty box."

Well, our company is in the penalty box now. But it was inevitable, if not this year, then soon. The earnings tightrope was too long and the market winds too high for us to meet their expectations. So let's not fight it. Let's exploit it. I think we should move away from managing the market's expectations and invest more time in building the analysts' understanding of the company and its fundamental economics. That means being much clearer about our strategy, what risks it entails, and what the analysts need to believe about us and our markets to think we're a good investment.

Now let *me* be clear: I'm not advocating that we simply do a better job of "investor relations"—at least as the term has been defined in recent years. I'm talking about basing our discussions with analysts on the fundamentals of our business. At present, we spend most of our time with them trying to predict our quarterly earnings down to the very last penny. Last year, we forecast annual earnings within a range of 20 cents per share. Given the previous year's earnings of $2.25 per share, we were offering a number with roughly a 10% margin of error. How can we make such a forecast when we compete in a global business that has not only normal systemic risks but also competitive, product-liability, and exchange-rate risks, among others?

Instead of engaging in this virtually meaningless exercise, let's give the analysts a better understanding of the progress—or lack thereof—we're making on key strategic initiatives and then link that progress to future financial results. We currently do the opposite, obfuscating what's going on in the business to leave ourselves future flexibility. But if growth in a new product or gaining access to new channels is key to our success, then we need to be more forthcoming about how we're doing. It's not as if the analysts won't find out eventually. And I'm sure we can provide this information with enough discretion to avoid publishing anything a determined competitor couldn't find out independently.

By being more forthcoming, we can get analysts to focus on what we're actually managing—the business—and less on what we can't manage nearly as precisely—the quarter-to-quarter financial results. It will also relieve them of the burden of surmising the cause-and-effect relationship between our strategy and our financial results—and us of the burden of speaking to them obliquely. If nothing else, the analysts ought to be grateful, given the cloud that hangs over audited financial statements. If we get out in front on this, I think we have a real chance to differentiate ourselves from our competitors.

I THINK YOU'LL FIND an approach that features visible, accurate, and reliable information about corporate performance much more to the liking of the board, too. I've complained to you before that the senior executives seem to treat our strategy reviews with them like a

dinner at the in-laws. They're on their best behavior, say
as little as possible that might be remotely controversial,
and define victory as a clean getaway. I don't think the
more experienced directors like the degree to which we
have been shut out of substantive discussions. We all
know that you're cautious about inviting too much back-
and-forth. Indeed, all of us directors run or have run our
own outfits and know that too many cooks spoil the
soup. But you don't have to substitute pablum for soup.
If you adopt the type of discipline I'm suggesting you
adopt in your discussions with the Street, you will greatly
elevate the quality of the discussions we have in the
boardroom. You'll also have a board that adds more
value and is more committed to your program.

I should add that, at some point, it doesn't matter
what I prefer or what you think about the substance of
board meetings. Enron and WorldCom changed everything. I don't know of a single director of a publicly
traded company that hasn't reviewed his D&O insurance
policies in recent months. No one in his right mind is
going to put his reputation at risk by not knowing what
is really going on in companies whose shareholders he
represents. Just as shareholders should insist on a far
clearer line of sight between financial projections and
management actions, boards will insist on understanding the links between management decisions and business risk. Your board will certainly be one of them.

Let me turn to the senior executive team. I've been
concerned about where these managers have been focusing their attention in recent years. During last spring's
off-site, I chatted with many of them. They are bright
and motivated, no doubt. However, in my conversations
with them, each seemed unduly concerned about this
year's budget, making the quarter, and the market's reac-
tion to our recent "negative" earnings guidance.

Now, maybe that's what they thought I wanted to hear. And certainly, when I was in their shoes, I also was cautious about what I brought up with an outside director. But I think it's indicative of a more fundamental, and potentially insidious, problem. If we look at how these folks get paid, it should come as no surprise that they focus on the share price. In recent years, several things have happened. The tolerance for short-term performance problems has become almost nonexistent. And as an executive team and a board, we have consistently signaled to top managers that they had better make the numbers, or else. Why? Because we feel we have to make the earnings estimates, or else. And, by loading executives up with options, we guaranteed that they would focus on share-price performance as well.

Certainly, the Compensation Committee eagerly embraced this program as a vehicle for ensuring that executives focus on shareholder value. But I wonder now whether we actually accomplished that purpose. Should these people really be checking the hourly movement of the stock price at the expense of worrying about product marketing, the workforce, and asset utilization? Someday, once they have proven themselves at the business-unit and group-VP levels, they will find it important to monitor the health of the overall corporation, as reflected in the fluctuations in its stock price. For the moment, though, they should focus on those things they control directly.

Furthermore, it would seem to me that through our use of options we've infected top managers with the same type of short-term thinking that was the punch line of every joke about American management 15 years ago, when American executives were criticized for managing by the numbers and lacking any real sense of their business or industry. More importantly, I wonder if we've skewed their expectations. I realize that during the height of the dot-com bubble, everybody and his uncle believed their destiny was to get rich, young. We certainly accelerated the pace of salary and bonus increases to keep the best of our executives, when we feared they would head off to some new-economy start-up. Obviously, that fear has passed. Still, the aftereffects linger.

Don't get me wrong: As you know, I have argued in board meetings that there is a market for executives, and we have to meet that market to keep our top talent. You will credit me, I think, with being an unstinting ally in helping to maintain our position in the top quartile of executive compensation in our industry. While I think that is important, I don't think we should fall into a mindless, keeping-up-with-the-Joneses mentality. Every year, our compensation consultants tell us that the mean has shifted upward; every year, we meet the new standard. And, in recent years, that has meant not only increasing the number of options and broadening the group of recipients but also repricing them when our stock price fell. All of that added up to a huge shift in the expected value of our managers' compensation from salary and bonus to options. But after the battering our stock took during the tumultuous weeks the market experienced in the summer, we've shifted them on to thin ice. At this point, I don't think it's an overexaggeration to say that the fundamental, underlying logic of our executive compensation program is in tatters.

I think we need to revisit the logic of compensation for executives. We have to refocus them on their specific responsibilities by linking their individual rewards more materially to their performance in advancing our strategy. I'm not suggesting that we abandon shareholder value creation as our overarching metric. But I do think

we should start deconstructing that metric into component parts that are related to our strategy and reward
executives on that basis. Let's embed in the compensation system the same logic we'd like the market to adopt.

F INALLY, I BELIEVE we are fooling ourselves if we think
that the issues I have outlined above are lost on the
nonexecutive workforce. Just what have they seen from
us in the last five to ten years? First, they have witnessed a
massive increase in both the reported value of executive
pay packages and the amount of press coverage those
packages receive. More importantly, they have seen a fundamental change in the way we approach the business.
Simply put, they believe we lack commitment to it—and
to them. Many would call us not only selfish but spineless.
New product programs come and go, not on their merits,
but on our ability to fund them year to year based on
earnings requirements. Functions ranging from IT to
internal audit are outsourced, their employees unceremo-
niously seconded to new employers like so many inden-
tured servants. Procurement "rationalization" results in
the termination of longtime suppliers. Overhead cost
reduction campaigns, "delayering," and early retirement
incentive packages are followed by a massive ramp-up in
hiring—and then equally precipitous layoffs.

What message do these moves send to our employees? Basically, we're saying: "When the chips are down,
don't count on us." And that's a message that's not only
heartless but dangerous. I believe our employees want
the company to succeed and, on the whole, are willing to
put up with a lot to ensure that outcome. But they have
to be given some reason to make that sacrifice. We no
longer denominate success in building great products or

providing a great place to work, but in cents per share. Frankly, that is not enough.

Implicit in what I've been saying is the need for you to rethink how you exercise leadership in this company. Leading in a time of uncertainty is a fundamentally different task from leading in a time of unquestioned irrational exuberance. If we think about those leaders whose greatness evinces itself in times of trouble, what we remember is their ability to communicate. Their messages always share the same qualities—clarity, consistency, and an underlying moral purpose. Moreover, they demonstrate the integrity of those messages through their actions, setting a course and then staying with it in the face of adversity and opposition. In short, they say what they mean and do what they say.

Their messages may be delivered in the native dialects of their different constituencies; these leaders, after all, know their audiences. But the overarching theme is the same. And it embodies a mission that people can rally around.

Let's face it. You don't motivate people with "Let's knock ourselves out again to make another stretch quarter." As rallying cries go, this isn't exactly, "Once more unto the breach, dear friends!" To inspire people to follow you, to commit themselves to your endeavor, to make needed sacrifices, you have to offer an inspiring mission. It doesn't need to be dramatic, but it does need to be meaningful. I think restoring sound, strategic decision making that looks beyond tomorrow's analyst's report will take us a long way toward a mission of which we can all be proud.

The results will take care of themselves.

Originally published in October 2002
Reprint 1989

Countering the Biggest Risk of All

ADRIAN J. SLYWOTZKY AND JOHN DRZIK

Executive Summary

CORPORATE TREASURERS AND CHIEF financial officers have become adept at quantifying and managing a wide variety of risks: financial (for example, currency fluctuations), hazard (chemical spills), and operational (computer system failures). To defend themselves, they use tried-and-true tools such as hedging, insurance, and backup systems. Some companies have even adopted the concept of enterprise risk management, integrating available risk management techniques in a comprehensive, organization-wide approach. But most managers have not addressed in a systematic way the greatest threat of all–*strategic risks*, the array of external events and trends that can devastate a company's growth trajectory and shareholder value.

Strategic risks go beyond such familiar challenges as the possible failure of an acquisition or a product launch. A new technology may overtake your product. Gradual shifts in the market may slowly erode one of your brands beyond the point of viability. Or rapidly shifting customer priorities may suddenly change your industry. The key to surviving these strategic risks, the authors say, is knowing how to assess and respond to them.

In this article, they lay out a method for identifying and responding to strategic threats. They categorize the risks into seven major classes (industry, technology, brand, competitor, customer, project, and stagnation) and describe a particularly dangerous example within each category. The authors also offer countermeasures to take against these risks and describe how individual companies (American Express, Coach, and Air Liquide, among them) have deployed them to neutralize a threat and, in many cases, capitalize on it.

Besides limiting the downside of risk, strategic-risk management forces executives to think more systematically about the future, thus helping them identify opportunities for growth.

W HATEVER YOUR BUSINESS, consider for a moment the remarkable turnaround over the past decade in the U.S. banking industry. In the early 1990s, the industry—rocked by the Latin American debt crisis, a major real estate bust, and economic recession—suffered massive loan losses, erratic earnings, and the

highest rate of bank failures since the Depression. A
decade later, as much of the economy reeled from the
dot-com bust and another recession, banks were generally flourishing. The number of bad loans was down,
earnings were relatively stable, and the banking industry
was outperforming the market as a whole.

The turnaround occurred in large part because
banks were able to develop new tools and techniques
to counter risk, in the process giving birth to an entirely
new discipline of financial risk management. Sophisticated credit-scoring measures reduced banks' credit
losses. New forms of options, futures, and counterparty
agreements allowed banks to redistribute their financial
risks. In fact, banking regulations now require companies to employ financial models that quantify their
market risks.

We cite this example because the risks that plagued
banks 15 years ago are emblematic of the challenges that
companies across *all* industries increasingly face today.
What if these companies could also employ tools and
techniques that would provide some protection against
a broad set of high-stakes risks?

These looming threats form a category we call
strategic risk—that is, the array of external events and
trends that can devastate a company's growth trajectory
and shareholder value. The evidence of strategic risk is
becoming ever more apparent. In the past 20 years,
there has been a dramatic decrease in the number of
stocks receiving a high quality rating by Standard &
Poor's and a dramatic increase in the number of low-
quality stocks. (See the exhibit "A Hazardous Environment.") And our own analysis indicates that from 1993
through 2003, more than one-third of *Fortune* 1,000
companies—only a fraction of which were in volatile

high-technology industries—lost at least 60% of their value in a single year.

So how should a company respond to threats of this magnitude? The answer lies in devising and deploying a systematic approach to managing strategic risk.

Broadening the Focus

The discipline of risk management has made considerable progress in recent years. Corporate treasurers and chief financial officers have become adept at quantifying and managing a wide range of risks: financial (for example, currency fluctuations), hazard (chemical

---

A Hazardous Environment

One measure of the increased strategic risks companies face is the sharp drop in the percentage of the 3,000 S&P-rated stocks receiving a high quality rating (based on S&P's assessment of a company's ability to achieve long-term, stable earnings growth) and the increase in the percentage of stocks receiving a low quality rating. High-quality stocks include those rated A+, A, and A-. Low-quality stocks include those rated B, B-, C, and D. (B+ stocks are omitted.)

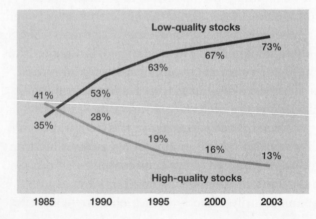

spills), and operational (computer system failures). They defend themselves against these risks through now tried-and-true tools such as hedging, insurance, and backup systems.

Spurred by the banking industry's success in financial risk management and by Sarbanes-Oxley's rigorous standards for corporate governance, some firms have been adopting the practice of "enterprise risk management," which seeks to integrate available risk management techniques in a comprehensive, organization-wide approach. Many of these early adopters are at a rudimentary stage, in which they treat enterprise risk management as an extension of their audit or regulatory compliance processes. Other companies are at a more advanced stage, in which they quantify risks and link them to capital allocation and risk-transfer decisions. Even among these more advanced practitioners, however, the focus of enterprise risk management rarely encompasses more than financial, hazard, and operational risks. Most managers have not yet systematically addressed the strategic risks that can be a much more serious cause of value destruction. (A method for assessing and responding to the strategic risks your company faces is presented in the insert "A Manager's Guide to Strategic Risk.")

Strategic risks take a variety of forms that go beyond such familiar challenges as the possible failure of an acquisition or a product launch. A new technology may overtake your product. (Think of how ACE inhibitors and calcium channel blockers stole share in the hypertension drug market from beta-blockers and diuretics.) Gradual shifts in the market may slowly erode one of your brands beyond the point of viability. (Recall the demise of the Oldsmobile brand.) Or rapidly shifting customer priorities may suddenly change your industry.

(Consider how quickly baby boomer parents migrated from station wagons to minivans, catching most automakers off guard.)

The key to surviving strategic risks is knowing how to assess and respond to them. Devoting the resources to do this is well worth it. Many companies already commit themselves to meticulously managing even relatively small risks—for instance, auditing their invoices to comply with new corporate governance regulations. These firms can realize even greater value by taking a disciplined and systematic approach to mitigating the strategic risks that can make or break them. Of course, no company can anticipate *all* risk events: There will always be unpreventable surprises that can damage your organization—which makes it all the more important to manage those risks that can be prevented.

Taking this stance promises benefits beyond just protecting your company's value. When a risk is common to all companies in an industry, taking early steps to mitigate it can put your business in a much stronger competitive position. Moreover, many strategic risks mask growth opportunities. By managing strategic risk, you can position your company as a risk *shaper* that is both more aggressive and more prudent in pursuing new growth. Such benefits make strategic-risk management a crucial capability both for chief financial officers who need to protect the stability of their companies and for any senior managers looking for sources of sustainable growth.

An Array of Risks and Countermeasures

We categorize strategic risk into seven major classes: industry, technology, brand, competitor, customer, project, and stagnation. Within each class, there are different types of risks. We will describe a particularly dangerous risk from each category and how individual companies have—or have not—deployed countermeasures to neutralize the threat and, in many cases, capitalize on it. (For a list of these risks and countermeasures, see the exhibit "Preventive Measures.")

INDUSTRY MARGIN SQUEEZE

As industries evolve, a succession of changes can unfold that threaten all companies in the sector. For example, it can become very costly to conduct R&D, as has

---

Preventive Measures

Companies face an array of strategic risks. Even the most serious, though, can be mitigated through the use of effective countermeasures.

Strategic Risk	Countermeasures
Industry margin squeeze	Shift the compete/collaborate ratio.
Technology shift	Double bet.
Brand erosion	Redefine the scope of brand investment. Reallocate brand investment.
One-of-a-kind competitor	Create a new, non-overlapping business design.
Customer priority shift	Create and analyze proprietary information. Conduct quick and cheap market experiments.
New-project failure	Engage in smart sequencing. Develop excess options. Employ the stepping-stone method.
Market stagnation	Generate "demand innovation."

---

happened in pharmaceuticals: The industry has experienced decreasing yield rates for new drugs, and companies are targeting more new therapies for chronic rather than acute diseases, which require larger and longer clinical trials. It can become costly to make capital expenditures, as has occurred in semiconductor fabrication: Costs have risen because of greater purity requirements, larger scale, and more complex equipment. An industry may go through rapid deregulation, like that experienced by airlines, which sharpens price competition among companies with high cost structures. Suppliers may gain power over their customers because of consolidation, which occurred among suppliers of flat-panel displays, or because of the suppliers' direct marketing to end users, which Intel did with its Intel Inside campaign. The industry may become subject to extreme business-cycle volatility, something experienced in telecommunications. Perhaps the greatest risk is that, because of a combination of these and other factors, such as overcapacity and commoditization, profit margins will be gradually destroyed for all players, and the entire industry will become a no-profit zone.

The most effective countermeasure to this squeeze on margins is *shifting the compete/collaborate ratio* among the relevant firms. When an industry is growing and margins are fat, companies can afford to compete on nearly all fronts and eschew collaboration. But this 100:0 ratio of competition to collaboration should rapidly shift when margins start to erode. Collaboration can take many forms without violating antitrust laws: the sharing of back-office functions, coproduction or asset-sharing agreements, purchasing and supply chain coordination, joint research and development, and collaborative marketing. Most companies, though, fail to respond to changes in the economics of an industry quickly enough, and collaboration begins too late to make a difference. Witness the recent history of airlines, utilities, textile manufacturers, steel makers, music production companies, and automakers.

Two notable exceptions to this too-little-too-late phenomenon are the Airbus consortium of European aircraft manufacturers and the Sematech consortium of U.S. semiconductor manufacturers, which played critical roles in helping their members regain market share and improve shrinking margins. Of course, both of these initiatives involved government participation, but that shouldn't be allowed to cloud the issue. The dispute between the United States and the European Union over whether Airbus has received unfair government subsidies, for example, has tended to overshadow the tremendous efficiencies the partnership has made possible. And there are numerous examples of collaboration with no government involvement. The Visa and MasterCard networks allow member financial institutions to share payment-processing and marketing services that are much more efficient than any one bank could hope to create on its own. The True Value organization gives independent hardware retailers access to marketing, purchasing, and loyalty programs that allow them to compete against national giants.

Contrast the success of those collaborations with the plight of major music production companies. After file sharing emerged and enabled the widespread downloading of music, the recording companies collectively suffered a decline in sales at an annual rate of 6.5% from 2000 through 2003. Collaboration became an economic imperative, but the music companies offered only a fragmented response. Universal and Sony launched a joint venture for selling music online called Pressplay, while Bertelsmann, EMI, and Warner Music Group worked with RealNetworks to launch Music-Net. The two services refused to license songs to each other, which reduced their appeal to customers, and neither captured enough paying customers to be viable. This left the field open to Apple's iTunes online music store. It convinced the recording companies not only that it had a workable copyright-protection scheme but that customers wanted to buy, not rent, individual songs. In its first eight months, iTunes grabbed more than one-third of the overall revenues from song downloads from the fractious recording companies.

TECHNOLOGY SHIFT

Risks involving technology—for example, the probability that a product will lose its patent protection or that a manufacturing process will become outdated—can have a major effect on corporate performance. But when a new technology unexpectedly invades a marketplace, specific product and service offerings may actually become obsolete in short order. Think, for example, of the way in which digital imaging has shifted market share away from film-based photography.

Of course, you often don't know how and when a technology will win acceptance in the marketplace or which version of a new technology will ultimately prevail. That's why risk-savvy managers faced with an unpredictable situation insure against technology risk by *double betting*—that is, investing in two or more versions of a technology simultaneously so they can thrive no matter which version emerges as the winner. Betting on both the OS/2 and the Windows operating systems

positioned Microsoft to be a winner, regardless of which
one prevailed. Intel's double bet on both RISC and CISC
chip architectures improved the firm's chances of suc-
ceeding in the semiconductor industry. By contrast,
Motorola's failure to pursue both analog and digital cel-
lular-phone technology opened the door for Nokia to
supplant it as the industry leader.

In fact, the cell phone market has experienced a series
of technology shifts over the past decade, each posing a
fresh challenge to the established companies. In 2002, for
example, Nokia decided to concentrate on high-end
smart phones and directed 80% of its R&D budget
toward this market—failing to double bet on moderately
priced phones. Rival Samsung capitalized on this and
invested heavily in midrange phones as part of its broad
portfolio of products. Midrange handsets took off in 2003
while smart phones fizzled, and Samsung enjoyed 32%
sales growth for the year, compared with 6% growth
for the overall cell phone market. Nokia's failure to
double bet in this case has presented the company with
a new strategic challenge against a powerful and committed rival, increasing the overall risk level of Nokia's
market position.

Of course, double betting often requires significant
short-term investments, so *how* you double bet is crucial.
In the late 1990s, the Internet's growth posed a classic
double-bet problem for financial services firms. Some
companies, such as Bank One, invested large sums in
building Internet banking channels, only to discover that
very few of their customers—and even fewer profitable
customers—wanted online-only service. Because the
Web sites were poorly coordinated with the companies'
traditional service departments, customers weren't able
to easily move from one channel to another, and the

banks' investments were largely wasted. Contrast that
ineffective double betting with how discount brokerage
firm Charles Schwab managed its Internet hedge.
Schwab integrated its new eSchwab portal into its existing service network, giving investors the freedom to
move from one channel to another—from the Web to
phones to personal visits with their brokers—as they
accessed account information and performed transactions. Subsequent market changes have challenged
Schwab's business model, but during the 1990s the
company was able to ride the wave of Internet-driven
growth because it double bet on competing customer
channels.

BRAND EROSION

Brands are subject to an array of risks, some predictable
and some not, that can sharply reduce their value. In
some cases, the risk can appear overnight and threaten
the brand with outright collapse. When some of Perrier's
bottled water was found to be contaminated, the company experienced a rapid and significant drop in market
share. And when some Firestone tires were deemed
defective, parent company Bridgestone suffered an 80%
drop in net income over one year. In other cases, the
relevance and attractiveness of a brand may erode
because of underinvestment or misdirected investment.
Think of the gradual decline of GM's Saturn brand when,
after a successful launch, the company failed to develop
new models fast enough to satisfy customers.

One of the most effective countermeasures to brand
erosion is *redefining the scope of brand investment*
beyond marketing, taking into account other factors
that affect a brand, such as service and product

quality. Another effective countermeasure involves the continuous *real-location of brand investment* based on early signs of weakness identified through constant measurement of the key dimensions of the brand.

That is how American Express averted the risk of brand erosion over the past decade. A pioneer in the charge card industry, Amex came under competitive attack in the late 1980s from Visa and several major banks, which began to take market share from Amex worldwide by challenging consumer perceptions of the Amex brand. Visa, in its advertising, emphasized merchants' wider acceptance of its card (". . . and they don't take American Express"), while the banks emphasized incentive programs that rewarded frequent usage. Amex's brand, built on prestige and service, was becoming too narrowly focused and less relevant in customers' eyes.

So Amex made a series of investments, some of them unrelated to conventional marketing, to strengthen and broaden the brand. To increase the number of service establishments accepting its cards, Amex invested in its relationships with merchants—reducing their transaction fees, speeding up payments, and increasing support for their advertising. The cut in transaction fees alone reduced Amex's revenues by about $170 million annually, but higher charge volumes more than made up for the loss. Amex also invested heavily in its Membership Miles rewards program, paying more to participating airlines and expanding the program to include five major hotel chains. This reallocation of investments arrested the brand's slide early and contributed to the company's dramatic growth in market value over the past decade.

ONE-OF-A-KIND COMPETITOR

A company's competitors, existing and potential, clearly
are one of the main sources of business risk, whether the
threat stems from a rival's new product or the emergence
of global competitors with lower cost structures. Perhaps
the most serious competitive risk, though, is that a one-
of-a-kind competitor will appear and seize the lion's
share of value in a market. It is vitally important to constantly scan the horizon to identify and track as early as
possible the companies that, whether in your industry or
not, could become such a rival. When you've identified
one, the best response is a rapid *change in business
design* that minimizes your strategic overlap with the
unique competitor and allows you to establish a profitable position in an adjacent economic space.

Any retailer tracking the proliferation of Wal-Mart
stores on a map of the United States during the 1980s
and 1990s would have been able to predict precisely
when this retailing tidal wave, driven by Wal-Mart's
unique business model, would wash through its home
territory. Many major retail chains failed to do so. A
handful, however, did respond in time, maintaining and
growing their value by shifting their business designs to
capture their own distinct slices of the market. Discount
retailer Target, in the early 1990s, identified the need
to offer a unique product selection to compete with
Wal-Mart's. In response, it recrafted itself from a conventional discounter to a low-price but style-conscious
retailer that appeals to a different customer set than
Wal-Mart's. By contrast, Family Dollar stores have
driven steady growth by targeting low- and fixed-
income households, offering basic household items,
food, and apparel in small, bare-bones stores throughout

neighborhoods that are too down-market, too rural, or too urban for Wal-Mart.

CUSTOMER PRIORITY SHIFT

Many strategic risks involve customers—a shift in the balance of power toward them and away from companies, for example, or companies' overreliance on a small number of customers. But perhaps the biggest risk is the shift—suddenly and dramatically or gradually and almost invisibly—in customers' preferences. Such shifts happen all the time; the magnitude of the risk depends on its speed, breadth, and depth.

Two powerful countermeasures for managing this risk are the continuous *creation and analysis of proprietary information*, which can detect the next phase of customer priorities, and *fast and cheap experimentation*, which helps managers to quickly home in on the right product variations to offer different customer microsegments. These methods can help companies retain and grow their customer bases—even as customers' preferences evolve—and, over time, increase revenue per customer and overall profitability.

One company that has rapidly become proficient in these methods is Coach, which makes high-quality leather goods. When Coach was spun off from Sara Lee in 2000, it trailed competitors Gucci and LVMH in revenue, profitability, and market capitalization. This was also a period of unanticipated growth and change at the sector's middle-market level, where purses, handbags, and briefcases sell, at retail, in the $200 to $400 range. Known for its conservative styling, Coach faced a high-risk situation as it tried to discern how long its existing customers would stick with the company if it ventured down the more trendy fashion paths that would allow it to expand its customer base. In the past four years, Coach has managed this risk well enough to surpass Gucci in revenue growth rate, profit margin, and market capitalization.

Some of this success can be attributed to Coach's aggressive in-market testing of new products—customer interviews (more than 10,000 a year), in-store product tests, and market experiments that record the effect of changing such variables as price, features, and offers by competing brands. Based on the proprietary information it gathers, Coach quickly alters product designs, drops items that test poorly, creates new lines in a wider range of fabrics and colors, changes prices, and tailors merchandise presentations to fit customer demographics at specific stores. Several years ago, Coach had customers preview its Hampton satchel and learned that they would willingly pay $30 more than the company had thought. In the case of another bag, Coach solicited customer feedback on the design and, learning that customers found it "tippy," responded by widening the base of the bag. As a result of such close and continuous customer contact, Coach has avoided numerous market misfires and has been able to maintain its popularity among its traditional fans while simultaneously attracting a new, younger generation of customers.

Although 10,000 individual customer interviews and the several million dollars a year that Coach spends on in-market testing may seem excessive, the investment of time and money represents a low-cost form of insurance against getting blindsided by customers' shifting priorities. And Coach isn't alone in its generation and smart use of proprietary customer data. A number of companies have developed information systems that keep them plugged in to the microsegments and constant micro-shifts of their customers. Those firms include Capital One, which conducts 65,000 in-market experiments per year to identify ever smaller customer segments in the credit card market, and Japanese video and music distributor Tsutaya, which analyzes customer spending patterns through point-of-sale data, surveys, and databases.

NEW-PROJECT FAILURE

Any project involves countless risks. A new product or service venture faces the chance that it won't work technically, that it will fail to attract profitable customers, that competitors will quickly copy it and poach market share, or that its growth will be too slow or too costly. There are also major financial and opportunity risks associated with a new marketing campaign, a major IT or R&D project, or a company acquisition. Indeed, the tough reality is that some four out of five new business projects fail.

The best protection against this risk begins with a clear-eyed assessment of a project's chance of success before it is launched—something that, as everyone knows from experience, often doesn't take place for any number of personal or organizational reasons. Once this evaluation is completed—for example, by reviewing data on past company projects or by collecting external data on the success rate of similar projects—three approaches can help a company systematically improve a project's odds. These are *smart sequencing*, which means undertaking the better-understood, more-controllable projects first; *developing excess options* when planning a project in order to improve the chances of eventually picking the best one; and *employing the stepping-stone method*, which means creating a series of projects that lead from uncertainty to success.

An example of a company using smart sequencing is semiconductor equipment maker Applied Materials, which has carefully focused on the stages of the chip-making process and mastered each stage before moving to another one. Chip making involves at least 15 different stages and some 450 discrete steps. Most equipment suppliers are involved in just one or two stages of the chip-making process. While no supplier is yet capable of providing all the tools needed to create a state-of-the-art semiconductor fabrication system, Applied Materials comes close. It started by selling equipment for one stage, chemical vapor deposition. Based on its understanding of that part of the chip-making process—including the economics of the process and the preferences of key decision makers—Applied Materials added capabilities in adjacent or related stages, such as ion implantation and etching. The company now makes products for 13 chip-making stages and is the leading company in most of its product markets. The risk of taking each step was reduced by the knowledge and customer relationships the company developed in the previous stage. Investors have rewarded Applied Materials for its smart sequencing: While the company's share of the semiconductor equipment industry's revenues is below 40%, its share of the industry's market value has remained between 50% and 60%.

Project failures loom large in the automotive industry, where enormous investments are required to retool plants and develop worldwide marketing, sales, and maintenance programs around a new vehicle. Hence the significance of Toyota's use of excess options in developing its gas-electric hybrid, the Prius. Toyota's process for creating the Prius was a seemingly wasteful one. As recounted by Jeffrey K. Liker in *The Toyota Way*, the company "overinvested" in the Prius by generating a proliferation of design options and then sifting through them to find the best ones. Rather than quickly focusing on a handful of good alternatives, the Prius team simultaneously tested 20 different suspension systems and examined 80 different hybrid engine technologies before focusing on four designs, each of which was then tested and refined in exhaustive detail.

Toyota also took a stepping-stone approach to rolling out the vehicle, a method well-known in the software industry, in which version 1.0 is full of errors, version 2.0 shows great improvement, and version 3.0 is a market success. Version 1 of the Prius, launched in Japan in 1997, was good enough to appeal to a solid base of customers eager to try hybrid technology. Version 2, launched in 2002, featured improved styling, interior space, handling, and fuel economy. There's still a months-long waiting list to buy version 2 of the Prius, which has captured 80% of the world hybrid automobile market, and Toyota now has other hybrid vehicles in development, including a version of the Lexus RX330, that promise to offer even better performance for customers.

MARKET STAGNATION

Countless great companies have seen their market value plateau or decline as a result of their inability to find new sources of growth. In some cases, they face a slowdown in volume growth in a mature market. In others, despite strong volume growth, prices fall and produce weak earnings. Even when the market is strong, an individual company's weak pipeline of products can produce persistent lackluster results.

The most effective countermeasure to the perennial problem of stagnating volume growth is *demand innovation*. This involves redefining your market by looking at it through the lens of the customers' economics and expanding the value you offer your customers beyond product functionality—that is, helping them reduce their costs, capital intensity, cycle time, and risk in order to improve their profitability.

During the past ten years, Air Liquide, a century-old, tradition-bound supplier of industrial gases, was able to pursue demand innovation in a flagging industry. The company, based in Paris, had always excelled at technical innovation. But by the late 1980s, its revenue and operating income were flat, and technical innovation was leading nowhere, until the company redirected its innovation efforts to help improve customers' systems economics.

In the early 1990s, Air Liquide developed technology that allowed customers to establish small gas production facilities on-site rather than rely on large centralized plants and tanker shipments for their energy. One important side effect of on-site production was the higher level of interaction between customers and the Air Liquide staff. The on-site teams soon discovered that their industrial customers had a variety of pressing needs that Air Liquide might be able to address—for example, minimizing the risk of environmental and safety violations and improving their production processes. Senior management began to see how the firm's R&D and production knowledge, which it had struggled to turn into meaningful product differentiation, could be harnessed to improve customers' industrial processes.

Air Liquide gradually expanded from its core commodity gas business to offer a set of new services that included chemicals management, supply chain services, environmental consulting, and the licensing of software tools and systems. By seizing these new opportunities, the company has expanded its potential markets, gained a greater share of its customers' spending, and improved customer profitability and loyalty. As a result, Air Liquide has delivered strong and consistent financial results since the mid-1990s.

The Upside of Risk

Basketball star Bill Russell was a great re-bounder, seizing control of the ball after an opposing player missed a shot. While rebounding is considered a defensive skill, Russell always insisted that "rebounding is the start of the offense." By the time Russell grabbed the ball, he was already thinking about the teammate to whom he would pass and, ultimately, the shot he was setting up. He was constantly turning a defensive move into an offensive opportunity.

Similarly, strategic risk management allows managers to move from defense to offense. People typically focus on the perils of risk, and the managerial response is to seek ways to minimize exposure to it. But the pursuit of growth requires companies to take risks, to place bets on specific products, channels, customer segments, and new business models. Strategic risk management, besides limiting the downside of risk, helps managers improve the odds of success behind those bets by forcing them to think more systematically about the future and helping them to identify opportunities for growth.

In fact, the greatest opportunities often are concealed within the defensive countermeasures we've discussed. For Airbus, shifting to a collaborative model as a way for its member companies to escape shrinking margins enabled it to gain market share until it became a true rival to Boeing. For American Express, the fundamental change in its brand investment mix, in response to threats from other bank cards, set off a decade of value growth at the firm. For Target, shifting its focus to a customer segment that was different from Wal-Mart's not only helped it sidestep the Wal-Mart juggernaut but also sparked profitable growth that is the envy of other retailers.

A new view of the relationship between risk and reward is thus emerging. While managers often see a trade-off between the two, creative risk management combined with a good business model can allow a company to improve in both areas. This shift is analogous to the evolution of thinking about the relationship between cost and quality. Thirty years ago, managers believed there was a trade-off in which higher quality meant higher cost. Pioneering Japanese manufacturers turned that thinking around by showing that improving the system could actually reduce costs while simultaneously raising standards of quality.

Similarly, the challenge for managers today is to help their companies move to a position of lower risks but higher financial returns. With the right mind-set and timely deployment of countermeasures such as those described here, companies can manage the full spectrum of risks they face and find that risk/reward sweet spot.

A Manager's Guide to Strategic Risk

YOUR ORGANIZATION FACES a unique set of strategic risks based on factors such as your industry, competitive position, sources of revenue and profit, and brand strengths. You can mitigate such risks by systematically identifying, assessing, and responding to them. This process can be conducted on its own or as the fourth component of an enterprise risk management system, alongside similar processes for managing financial, hazard, and operational risks.

Step 1

Identify and assess your risks. Consider the key risks you face in the seven main categories of strategic risk—industry, technology, brand, competitor, customer, project, and stagnation—as well as the risks that may be specific to your industry or business model. For each type, consider:

- **Severity.** What percentage of your company's value could be affected by the risk? Consider previous analogous events in your industry or in other industries, as well as factors specific to your business that could increase or reduce the risk's impact—say, your organization's ability to adapt to external change.

- **Probability.** What's the likelihood of the risk occurring? Consider previous cases of companies affected by this risk; input from key customers, leading-edge customers, and other external influencers; and external data about probability rates.

- **Timing.** Can you determine when the risk is likely to occur? Maybe the timing has been predetermined, as in the case of patent expirations or regulatory changes. Or maybe you can estimate the time period during which the risk's impact will be greatest.
- **Changing probability over time.** Can you determine whether the likelihood of the risk is increasing, decreasing, or constant? For instance, the risk of a sharp decline in sales volume often increases in the fifth year of a business-cycle expansion. By contrast, the risk that a project will fail decreases as successive milestones for the project are met.

Step 2

Map your risks. Having identified and assessed your main risks, map them so you can see your profile at a glance. The exhibit "A Strategic Risk Map" lays out the risks faced by a hypothetical manufacturing and services firm. (You can fill in the blank lines with risks specific to your business.)

Step 3

Quantify your risks. Risks should be comprehensively measured in a common currency—for instance, cash flow at risk, earnings at risk, economic capital at risk, or market value at risk. Companies will then be able to compare and aggregate the risks and link them to decisions regarding capital allocation, pricing, and risk transfer.

Step 4

Identify the potential upside for each risk. What could happen if a key risk is reversed? For example, while your company could lose big by not double betting as technology changes, making two well-placed bets could create significant growth opportunities. Your company can develop a plan to identify and maximize the upside for each item listed in the strategic risk map.

Step 5

Develop risk mitigation action plans. For every major risk identified, there should be a team responsible for preparing a formal mitigation plan. This document will outline the risk assessments made in earlier steps (nature of the risk, root causes, percentage of market value that would be affected, and so on) and assign responsibility for executing countermeasures. The team will often need to be multifunctional. A brand risk, for example, may need to be managed by a team that includes representatives from marketing, customer service, and manufacturing.

Step 6

Adjust your capital decisions accordingly. After drawing up an explicit profile of the risks it faces, a company may want to change its capital calculations in two ways. First, business units and certain major projects that face greater levels of risk may warrant a higher cost of capital, one that's closer to venture-capital discount rates than typical corporate capital rates. Second, the company may need to change its capital structure depending on the way the risk level of the overall portfolio is changing over time. For instance, a company entering a

A Strategic Risk Map

The threats faced by a hypothetical manufacturing and services firm.

Type of Risk	Severity (% of Earnings at Stake)	Probability	Expected Timing in Years 1 2 3 4 5					Changing Probability Over Time
INDUSTRY								
Margin squeeze	80%	20%						Increasing
Rising R&D/capital expenditure costs	10%	40%						Increasing
Overcapacity								
Commoditization								
Deregulation								
Increased power among suppliers								
Extreme business-cycle volatility								
Other:								
TECHNOLOGY								
Shift in technology	60%	20%						Increasing
Patent expiration	10%	100%						Constant
Process becomes obsolete								
Other:								
BRAND								
Erosion	40%	20%						Increasing
Collapse	70%	10%						Constant
Other:								

COMPETITOR

Emerging global rivals	40%	20% Increasing
Gradual market-share gainer		
One-of-a-kind competitor	30%	5% Increasing
Other:		

CUSTOMER

Customer priority shift	20%	60% Increasing
Increasing customer power	10%	50% Increasing
Overreliance on a few customers		
Other:		

PROJECT

R&D failure	10%	80% Constant
IT failure		
Business-development failure		
Merger or acquisition failure		
Other:		

STAGNATION

Flat or declining volume	20%	80% Increasing
Volume up, price down		
Weak pipeline		
Other:		

period of greater volatility might need to become more conservative about capital, lowering its customary debt levels on its balance sheet or using joint ventures or other partnerships to spread the costs of a major new project.

Originally published in April 2005
Reprint 977X

A Framework for
Risk Management

KENNETH A. FROOT, DAVID S.
SCHARFSTEIN, AND JEREMY C. STEIN

Executive Summary

IN RECENT YEARS, managers have become
aware of how their companies can be buffeted by
risks beyond their control. Fluctuations in economic
and financial variables such as exchange rates,
interest rates, and commodity prices have often
had destabilizing effects on corporate strategies
and performance. To insulate themselves from such
risks, many companies are turning to the derivatives
markets, taking advantage of instruments like forwards, futures, options, and swaps.

Although heavily involved in risk management,
most companies do not have clear goals underlying their hedging programs. Without such goals,
using derivatives can be dangerous.

Kenneth Froot, David Scharfstein, and Jeremy Stein present a framework to guide top-level managers in developing a coherent risk-management strategy. That strategy cannot be delegated to the corporate treasurer—let alone to a hotshot financial engineer. Ultimately, a company's risk-management strategy needs to be integrated with its overall corporate strategy.

The authors' risk-management paradigm rests on three premises: (1) the key to creating corporate value is making good investments; (2) the key to making good investments is generating enough cash internally to fund them; (3) cash flow can often be disrupted by movements in external factors, potentially compromising a company's ability to invest. Therefore, a risk-management program should have one overarching goal: to ensure that a company has the cash available to make value-enhancing investments.

In RECENT YEARS, managers have become increasingly aware of how their organizations can be buffeted by risks beyond their control. In many cases, fluctuations in economic and financial variables such as exchange rates, interest rates, and commodity prices have had destabilizing effects on corporate strategies and performance. Consider the following examples:

- In the first half of 1986, world oil prices plummeted by 50%; overall, energy prices fell by 24%. While this was a boon to the economy as a whole, it was disastrous for oil producers as well as for companies like Dresser Industries, which supplies machinery and equipment to energy producers. As domestic oil production collapsed, so did demand for Dresser's equipment. The company's operating profits dropped from $292 million in 1985 to $139 million in 1986; its stock price fell from $24 to $14; and its capital spending decreased from $122 million to $71 million.

- During the first half of the 1980s, the U.S. dollar appreciated by 50% in real terms, only to fall back to its starting point by 1988. The stronger dollar forced many U.S. exporters to cut prices drastically to remain competitive in global markets, reducing short-term profits and long-term competitiveness. Caterpillar, the world's largest manufacturer of earthmoving equipment, saw its real-dollar sales decline by 45% between 1981 and 1985 before increasing by 35% as the dollar weakened. Meanwhile, the company's capital expenditures fell from $713 million to $229 million before jumping to $793 million in 1988. But by that time, Caterpillar had lost ground to foreign competitors such as Japan's Komatsu.

In principle, both Dresser and Caterpillar could have insulated themselves from energy-price and exchange-rate risks by using the derivatives markets. Today more and more companies are doing just that. The General Accounting Office reports that between 1989 and 1992 the use of derivatives—among them forwards, futures, options, and swaps—grew by 145%. Much of that growth came from corporations: one recent study shows a more than fourfold increase between 1987 and 1991 in their use of some types of derivatives.[1]

In large part, the growth of derivatives is due to innovations by financial theorists who, during the 1970s,
developed new methods—such as the Black-Scholes
option-pricing formula—to value these complex instruments. Such improvements in the technology of financial
engineering have helped spawn a new arsenal of risk-
management weapons.

Unfortunately, the insights of the financial engineers
do not give managers any guidance on how to deploy
the new weapons most effectively. Although many
companies are heavily involved in risk management,
it's safe to say that there is no single, well-accepted set
of principles that underlies their hedging programs.
Financial managers will give different answers to
even the most basic questions: What is the goal of risk
management? Should Dresser and Caterpillar have
used derivatives to insulate their stock prices from
shocks to energy prices and exchange rates? Or should
they have focused instead on stabilizing their near-term
operating income, reported earnings, and return on
equity, or on removing some of the volatility from their
capital spending?

Without a clear set of risk-management goals, using
derivatives can be dangerous. That has been made abun-
dantly clear by the numerous cases of derivatives trades
that have backfired in the last couple of years. Procter &
Gamble's losses in customized interest-rate derivatives
and Metallgesellschaft's losses in oil futures are two of
the most prominent examples. The important point is
not that these companies lost money in derivatives,
because even the best risk-management programs will
incur losses on some trades. What's important is that
both companies lost substantial sums of money—in the
case of Metallgesellschaft, more than $1 *billion*—because

they took positions in derivatives that did not fit well with their corporate strategies.

Our goal in this article is to present a framework to guide top-level managers in developing a coherent risk-management strategy—in particular, to make sensible use of the risk-management firepower available to them through financial derivatives.[2] Contrary to what senior managers may assume, a company's risk-management strategy cannot be delegated to the corporate treasurer—let alone to a hotshot financial engineer. Ultimately, a company's risk-management strategy needs to be integrated with its overall corporate strategy.

Our risk-management paradigm rests on three basic premises:

- The key to creating corporate value is making good investments.

- The key to making good investments is generating enough cash internally to fund those investments; when companies don't generate enough cash, they tend to cut investment more drastically than their competitors do.

- Cash flow—so crucial to the investment process—can often be disrupted by movements in external factors such as exchange rates, commodity prices, and interest rates, potentially compromising a company's ability to invest.

A risk-management program, therefore, should have a single overarching goal: to ensure that a company has the cash available to make value-enhancing investments.

By recognizing and accepting this goal, managers will be better equipped to address the most basic questions of risk management: Which risks should be hedged and which should be left unhedged? What kinds of

instruments and trading strategies are appropriate?
How should a company's risk-management strategy be
affected by its competitors' strategies?

From Pharaoh to Modern Finance

Risk management is not a modern invention. The Old
Testament tells the story of the Egyptian Pharaoh who
dreamed that seven healthy cattle were devoured by
seven sickly cattle and that seven healthy ears of corn
were devoured by seven sickly ears of corn. Puzzled by
the dream, Pharaoh called on Joseph to interpret it.
According to Joseph, the dream foretold seven years of
plenty followed by seven years of famine. To hedge
against that risk, Pharaoh bought and stored large quan-
tities of corn. Egypt prospered during the famine, Joseph
became the second most powerful man in Egypt, the
Hebrews followed him there, and the rest is history.

In the Middle Ages, hedging was made easier by the
creation of futures markets. Rather than buying and
storing crops, consumers could ensure the availability
and price of a crop by buying it for delivery at a predetermined price and date. And farmers could hedge the risk
that the price of their crops would fall by selling them for
later delivery at a predetermined price.

It is easy to see why Pharaoh, the consumer, and the
farmer would want to hedge. The farmer's income, for
example, is tied closely to the price he can get for his
crop. So any risk-averse farmer would want to insure his
income against fluctuations in crop prices just as many
working people protect their incomes with disability
insurance. It's not surprising, then, that the first futures
markets were developed to enable farmers to insure
themselves more easily.

More recently, large publicly held companies have emerged as the principal users of risk-management instruments. Indeed, most new financial products are designed to enable corporations to hedge more effectively. But, unlike the farmer, the consumer, and Pharaoh, it is not so clear why a *corporation* would want to hedge. After all, corporations are generally owned by many small investors, each of whom bears only a small part of the risk. In fact, Adolf A. Berle, Jr., and Gardiner C. Means argue in their classic book, *The Modern Corporation and Private Property*, that the modern corporate form of organization was developed precisely to enable entrepreneurs to disperse risk among many small investors. If that is true, it's hard to see why corporations themselves also need to reduce risk—investors can manage risk on their own.

Until the 1970s, finance specialists accepted this logic. The standard view was that if an investor does not want to be exposed to, say, the oil-price risk inherent in owning Dresser Industries, he can hedge for himself. For example, he can offset any loss on his Dresser Industries stock that might come from a decline in oil prices by also holding the stocks of companies that generally benefit from oil-price declines, such as petrochemical firms. There is thus no reason for the corporation to hedge on behalf of the investor. Or, put somewhat differently, hedging transactions at the corporate level sometimes lose money and sometimes make money, but on average they break even: companies can't systematically make money by hedging. Unlike individual risk management, corporate risk management doesn't hurt, but it also doesn't help.

Corporate finance specialists will recognize this logic as a variant of the Modigliani and Miller theorem, which was developed in the 1950s and became the foundation of "modern finance." The key insight of Franco Modigliani and Merton Miller, each of whom won a Nobel Prize for his work in this area, is that value is created on the left-hand side of the balance sheet when companies make good *investments*—in, say, plant and equipment, R&D, or market share—that ultimately increase operating cash flows. How companies finance those investments on the right–hand side of the balance sheet—whether through debt, equity, or retained earnings—is largely irrelevant. These decisions about financial policy can affect only how the value created by a company's real investments is divided among its investors. But in an efficient and well-functioning capital market, they cannot affect the overall value of those investments.

If one accepts the view of Modigliani and Miller, it follows almost as a corollary that risk-management strategies are also of no consequence. They are purely financial transactions that don't affect the value of a company's operating assets. Indeed, once the transaction costs associated with hedging instruments are factored in, a hard-line Modigliani-Miller disciple would argue against doing any risk management at all.

Over the past two decades, however, a different view of financial policy has emerged that allows a more integral role for risk management. This "postmodern" paradigm accepts as gospel the key insight of Modigliani and Miller—that value is created only when companies make good investments that ultimately increase their operating cash flows. But it goes further by treating financial policy as critical in *enabling* companies to make valuable investments. And it recognizes that companies face real trade-offs in how they finance their investments.[3]

For example, suppose a company wants to add a new plant that would expand its production capacity. If the company has enough retained earnings to pay for the cost of the plant, it will use those funds to build it. But if the company doesn't have the cash, it will need to raise capital from one of two sources: the debt market (perhaps through a bank loan or a bond issue) or the equity market.

It is unlikely that the company would decide to issue equity. Indeed, on average, less than 2% of all corporate financing comes from the external equity market.[4] Why the aversion to equity? The problem is that it's difficult for stock market investors to know the real value of a company's assets. They may get it right on average, but sometimes they price the stock too high and sometimes they price it too low. Naturally, companies will be reluctant to raise funds by selling stock when they think their equity is undervalued. And if they do issue equity, it will send a strong signal to the stock market that they think their shares are overvalued. In fact, when companies issue equity, the stock price tends to fall by about 3%.[5] The result: most companies perceive equity to be a costly source of financing and tend to avoid it.

The information problems that limit the appeal of equity are of much less concern when it comes to debt: most debt issues—particularly those of investment-grade companies—are easy to value even without precise knowledge of the company's assets. As a result, companies are usually less worried about paying too high an interest rate on their borrowings than about getting too low a price for their equity. It's therefore not surprising that the bulk of all external funding is from the debt market.

However, debt financing is not without cost: taking on too much debt limits a company's ability to raise funds later. No one wants to lend to a company with a large debt burden, because the company may use some of the new funds not to invest in productive assets but to pay off the old debt. In the extreme, high debt levels can trigger distress, defaults, and even bankruptcy. So while companies often borrow to finance their investments, there are limits to how much they can or will borrow.

The bottom line is that financial markets do not work as smoothly as Modigliani and Miller envisioned. The costs we have outlined make external financing of any form—be it debt or equity—more expensive than internally generated funds. Given those costs, companies prefer to fund investments with retained earnings if they can. In fact, there is a financial pecking order in which companies rely first on retained earnings, then on debt, and, as a last resort, on outside equity.

What is even more striking is that companies see external financing as so costly that they actually cut investment spending when they don't have the internally generated cash flow to finance all their investment projects. Indeed, one study found that companies reduced their capital expenditures by roughly 35 cents for each $1 reduction in cash flow.[6] These financial frictions thus determine not only how companies finance their investments but also whether they are able to undertake those investments in the first place. Internally generated cash is therefore a competitive weapon that effectively reduces a company's cost of capital and facilitates investment.

This is the most critical implication of the postmodern paradigm, and it forms the theoretical foundation of the view stated earlier—that the role of risk management is to ensure that companies have the cash available to make value-enhancing investments. Although the practical implications of this idea may seem vague, we will demonstrate how it can help to develop a coherent risk-management strategy.

Why Hedge?

Let's start with the case of a hypothetical multinational pharmaceutical company, Omega Drug. Omega's head-quarters, production facilities, and research labs are in the United States, but roughly half of its sales come from abroad, mainly Japan and Germany. Omega has several products that are still protected by patents, and it does not expect to introduce any new products this year. Omega's main uncertainty is the revenue it will receive from foreign sales. The company can forecast its foreign sales volume very accurately, but the dollar value of those sales is hard to pin down because of the uncertainty inherent in exchange rates. If exchange rates remain stable, Omega expects the dollar value of its cash flow from foreign and domestic operations to be $200 million. If, however, the dollar appreciates substantially relative to the Japanese yen and the German mark, then Omega's cash flow will fall to $100 million, since the weaker yen and mark mean that foreign cash flows are worth less in dollars. Conversely, a significant dollar depreciation would increase Omega's cash flow to $300 million. Each of these scenarios is equally likely.

Like most multinational corporations, Omega frequently receives calls from investment bankers trying to persuade the company to hedge its foreign-exchange risk. The bankers typically present an impressive set of calculations showing how Omega can reduce the risk in its earnings, cash flow, stock price, and return on equity simply by trading on foreign-exchange markets. So far,

Omega has resisted those overtures and has chosen not to engage in any substantial foreign-exchange hedging. "After all," Omega's top-level officers have argued, "we're a pharmaceutical company, not a bank."

Omega has one thing going for it: a healthy skepticism of bankers trying to sell their financial services. But the bankers also have something going for them: the skills to insulate companies from financial risk. What neither the company nor the bankers have is a well-articulated view of the role of risk management.

The starting point for our analysis is understanding the link between Omega's cash flows and its strategic investments, principally its R&D program. R&D is the key to success in the pharmaceutical business, and its importance has grown dramatically during the last two decades. Twenty years ago, Omega was spending 8% of sales on R&D; now it is spending 12% of sales on R&D.

Last year, Omega's R&D budget was $180 million. In the coming year, the company would like to spend $200 million. Omega arrived at this figure by first forecasting the increase in patentable products that would result from a particular level of R&D. As a second step, managers valued the increased cash flows through a discounted-cash-flow analysis. Such an approach could generate only rough estimates of the value of R&D because of the uncertainty inherent in the R&D process, but it was the best Omega could do. Specifically, the company's calculations indicated that an R&D budget of $200 million would generate a net present value of $90 million, compared with $60 million for R&D budgets of $100 million and $300 million. (See the exhibit "Payoffs from Omega Drug's R&D Investment.") The company took comfort in the knowledge that the $200 million budget was, on a relative basis, roughly in line with the budgets of its principal competitors.

Given its comparatively high leverage and limited collateral, Omega is not in a position to borrow any funds to finance its R&D program. It is also reluctant to issue equity. That leaves internally generated cash as the only funding source that Omega's managers are prepared to tap for the R&D program. Therefore, fluctuations in the dollar's exchange rate can be critical. If the dollar appreciates, Omega will have a cash flow of only $100 million to allocate to its R&D program—well below the desired $200 million budget. A stable dollar will generate enough cash flow for the program, while a depreciating dollar will generate an excess of $100 million. (See the exhibit "The Effect of Hedging on Omega Drug's R&D Investment and Value.")

Will Omega be better off if it hedges? Suppose Omega tells its bankers to trade on its behalf so that the company's cash flows are completely insulated from foreign-exchange risk. If the dollar appreciates, the trades will generate a $100 million gain; if the dollar depreciates, they'll post a $100 million loss. The trades will generate no gain or loss if the dollar remains at its current level. Effectively, the hedging program locks in net cash flows of $200 million for Omega—the cash flows that the

Payoffs from Omega Drug's R&D Investment

R&D Level*	Discounted Cash Flows*	Net Present Value*
100	160	60
200	290	90
300	360	60

*in millions of dollars

company would receive at prevailing exchange rates. Whatever the exchange rate turns out to be, Omega will have $200 million available for R&D—just the right amount.

If Omega doesn't hedge, it will be able to invest only $100 million in R&D if the dollar appreciates. By hedging, Omega is able to add $100 million of R&D in this scenario, increasing discounted future cash flows by $130 million (from $160 million to $290 million). On the other hand, if the dollar *depreciates*, Omega will lose $100 million on its foreign-exchange transactions. However, the $130 million gain clearly outweighs the $100 million loss. Overall, Omega is better off if it hedges.

Although this example is highly stylized, it illustrates a basic principle. In general, the supply of internally generated funds does not equal the investment demand for funds. Sometimes there is an excess supply; sometimes there is a shortage. Because external financing is costly, this imbalance shifts investment away from the optimal level. Risk management can reduce this imbalance and the resulting investment distortion. It enables companies to better align their demand for funds with their

The Effect of Hedging on Omega Drug's R&D Investment and Value

The Dollar	Internal Funds*	R&D Without Hedging*	Hedge Proceeds*	Additional R&D from Hedging*	Value from Hedging*
Appreciation	100	100	+100	100	+130
Stable	200	200	0	0	0
Depreciation	300	200	−100	0	−100

*in millions of dollars

internal supply of funds. That is, risk management lets companies transfer funds from situations in which they have an excess supply to situations in which they have a shortage. In essence, it allows companies to borrow from themselves.

Here's another way to look at what happens. As the dollar depreciates, the internal supply of funds—Omega's cash flow—increases. The demand for funds—the desired level of investment—is fixed and independent of the exchange rate. When the company doesn't hedge, demand and supply are equal only if the dollar remains stable. If the dollar depreciates, however, supply exceeds demand; if it appreciates, supply falls short of demand. By hedging, the company reduces supply when there is excess supply and increases supply when there is a shortage. This aligns the internal supply of funds with the demand for funds. Of course, the average supply of funds doesn't change with hedging, because hedging is a zero-net-present-value investment: it does not create value by itself. But it ensures that the company has the funds precisely when it needs them. Because value is ultimately created by making sure the company undertakes the right investments, risk management adds real value. (See the exhibit "Omega Drug: Hedging with Fixed R&D Investment.")

When to Hedge—or Not

The basic principle outlined above is just a first step. The real challenge of risk management is to apply it to developing strategies that deal with the variety of risks faced by different companies.

What we have argued so far is that companies should use risk management to align their internal supply of funds with their demand for funds. In the case of Omega Drug, that means hedging all the exchange-rate risk. Since we have assumed that the demand for funds—the desired amount of investment—isn't affected by exchange rates, Omega should stabilize its supply by insulating its cash flows from any changes in exchange rates. This assumption may be reasonable in the case of Omega because it is unlikely that the value of investing

Omega Drug: Hedging with Fixed R&D Investment

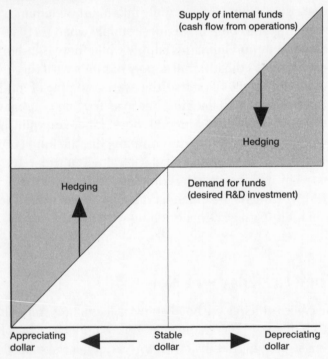

in R&D in pharmaceuticals would depend very much on exchange rates. But there are many instances in which exchange rates, commodity prices, or interest rates *do* affect the value of a company's investment opportunities. Understanding the connection between a company's investment opportunities and those key economic variables is critical to developing a coherent risk-management strategy.

Take the case of an oil company. The main risk it faces is changes in the price of oil. When oil prices fall, cash flows decline because existing oil properties produce less revenue. Therefore, the company's supply of internal funds is exposed to oil-price risk in much the same way that a multinational drug company's cash flows are exposed to foreign-exchange risk.

However, while the value of pharmaceutical R&D investment is unaffected by exchange rates, the value of investing in the oil business falls when oil prices drop. When prices are low, it's less attractive to explore for and develop new oil reserves. So when the supply of funds is low, so is the demand for funds. On the flip side, when oil prices rise, cash flows rise and the value of investing rises. Supply and demand are both high. For an oil company, much more than for a pharmaceutical company, the supply of funds tends to match the demand for funds even if the company does not actively manage risk. As a result, there is less reason for an oil company to hedge than there is for a multinational pharmaceutical company.

To illustrate the difference more clearly, let's change some of the numbers in our Omega Drug example and rename the company Omega Oil. Let's suppose there are three possible oil prices—low, medium, and high—which generate cash flows of $100 million, $200 million, and $300 million, respectively. The higher the oil price, the more revenue Omega Oil generates on its existing reserves.

So far, the example is exactly the same as before. Where it differs is on the investment side. The optimal amount of investment in the low-oil-price regime is $150 million; in the medium-oil-price regime, it's $200 million; and in the high-oil-price regime, it's $250 million. Thus, higher oil prices make exploring for and developing oil reserves more attractive. In this example, the supply of funds is not too far off from the demand for funds even if Omega Oil doesn't hedge. Omega Oil sometimes has an excess demand of $50 million and sometimes an excess supply of $50 million; with Omega Drug, the excess demand and excess supply were $100 million. Omega Oil, therefore, doesn't need to hedge its oil-price risk as much as Omega Drug needed to hedge its foreign-exchange risk. Roughly speaking, the optimal hedge for Omega Oil is only half that for Omega Drug.

Here the demand for funds increases with the price of oil. (See the graph "Omega Oil: Hedging with Oil-Price-Sensitive Investment.") The difference between supply and demand is smaller in the example of the oil company than it is when the investment level is fixed, as it was with Omega Drug. To align supply with demand, Omega Oil doesn't need to hedge as much as Omega Drug did. Essentially, Omega Oil already has something of a built-in hedge.

An important point emerges from this example: A proper risk-management strategy ensures that companies have the cash when they need it for investment, but it does not seek to insulate them completely from risks of all kinds.

If Omega Oil follows our recommended strategy and hedges oil-price risk only partially, then its stock price, earnings, return on equity, and any number of other performance measures will fluctuate with the price of oil. When oil prices are low, Omega is worth less: the company's existing properties are less valuable, and it will invest less. It's simply less profitable to be in the oil business, and this will be reflected in Omega's performance measures. But there's nothing a risk-management program can do to improve the underlying bad economics of low oil prices. The goal of risk management is not to insure investors and corporate managers against oil-price risk per se. It is to ensure that companies

Omega Oil: Hedging with Oil-Price-Sensitive Investment

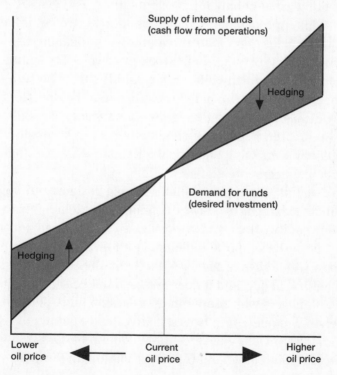

have the cash they need to create value by making good investments.

In fact, attempting to insulate investors completely from oil-price risk could actually *destroy* value. For example, if Omega Oil were to hedge fully, it would actually have an excess supply of funds when oil prices fall: its cash flow would be stabilized at $200 million, and its investment needs would be only $150 million. But when oil prices are high, just the opposite would be true: the company would lose so much money on its hedging position that it would have a shortage of funds for investment. Its net cash flows would still be only $200 million, but its investment needs would rise to $250 million. In this case, hedging fully would prevent the company from making value-enhancing investments.

This approach helps managers address two key issues. First, it helps them identify what is worth hedging and what isn't. Worrying about stock-price volatility in and of itself isn't worthwhile; such volatility can be better managed by individual investors through their portfolio strategies. By contrast, excessive *investment* volatility can threaten a company's ability to meet its strategic objectives and, as a result, is worth controlling through risk management.

Second, this approach helps managers figure out how much hedging is necessary. If changes in exchange rates, commodity prices, and interest rates lead to large imbalances in the supply and demand for funds, then the company should hedge aggressively; if not, the company has a natural hedge, and it does not need to hedge as much.

Managers who adopt our approach should ask themselves two questions: How sensitive are cash flows to risk variables such as exchange rates, commodity prices, and interest rates? and How sensitive are investment opportunities to those risk variables? The answers will help managers understand whether the supply of funds and the demand for funds are naturally aligned or whether they can be better aligned through risk management.

Guidelines for Managers

What follow are some guidelines for how managers can think about risk-management issues. Although these are by no means the only issues to consider, our suggestions should provide managers with useful direction.

Companies in the same industry should not necessarily adopt the same hedging strategy. To understand why, take the case of oil. Even though all oil companies are exposed to oil-price risk, some may be exposed more than others in both their cash flows and their investment opportunities. Let's compare Omega Oil with Epsilon Oil. Omega has existing reserves in Saudi Arabia that are a relatively cheap source of oil, whereas Epsilon gets its oil from the North Sea, which is a relatively expensive source. If the price of oil falls dramatically, Epsilon may be forced to shut down those reserves altogether, wiping out an important source of its cash flow. Omega would continue to operate its reserves because the cost of taking the oil out of the ground is still less than the oil price. Therefore, Epsilon's cash flows are more sensitive to the price of oil. Hedging is more valuable for Epsilon than it is for Omega because Epsilon's supply of funds is less in sync with its demand for funds.

Similar logic applies when the two oil companies differ in their investment opportunities. Suppose instead that Omega and Epsilon both have essentially the same cash-flow streams from their existing oil properties, but Epsilon is trying to develop new reserves in the North Sea, and Omega in Saudi Arabia. When the price of oil drops, it may no longer be worthwhile to try to develop reserves in the North Sea, since it is an expensive source of oil, but it may be worthwhile to do so in Saudi Arabia. Thus, the drop in the oil price affects both companies' cash flows equally, but Epsilon's investment opportunities fall more than Omega's do. Because Epsilon's demand for funds is more in line with its supply of funds, Epsilon has less incentive to hedge than Omega does.

Again, a simple message emerges: To develop a coherent risk-management strategy, companies must carefully articulate the nature of both their cash flows and their investment opportunities. Once they have done this, their efforts to align the supply of funds with the demand for funds will generate the right strategies for managing risk.

Companies may benefit from risk management even if they have no major investments in plant and equipment. We define investment very broadly to include not just conventional investments such as capital expenditures but also investments in intangible assets such as a well-trained workforce, brand-name recognition, and market share.

In fact, companies that make these sorts of investments may need to be even more active about managing risk. After all, a capital-intensive company can use its newly purchased plant and equipment as collateral to secure a loan. "Softer" investments are harder to collateralize. It may not be so easy for a company to raise capital from a bank to fund, say, short-term losses that result from a policy of pricing low to build market share. For companies that make such investments, internally generated funds are especially important. As a result, there may be an even greater need to align the supply of funds with the demand for funds through risk management.

Even companies with conservative capital structures—no debt, lots of cash—can benefit from hedging. At first glance, it might appear that a company with a very conservative capital structure should be less interested in risk management. After all, such a company could adjust rather easily to a large drop in cash flow by borrowing at relatively low cost. It wouldn't need to curtail investment, and corporate value would not suffer much. The basic objective of risk management—aligning the supply of internal funds with the demand for investment funding—has less urgency in this type of situation because managers can easily adjust to a supply shortfall by borrowing. To be sure, hedging wouldn't hurt, but it might not help much either.

But managers in this position should ask themselves why they have chosen such a conservative capital structure. If the answer is, The world is a risky place, and you never know what can happen to exchange rates or interest rates, they have more thinking to do. What they have done is use low leverage instead of, say, the derivatives markets to protect against the risk in those economic variables. An alternative strategy would be to take on more debt and then hedge those risks directly in the derivatives markets. In fact, there's something to be said for the second approach: it's no more risky in terms of the ability to make good investments than the low-debt/no-hedging strategy, but, in many countries, the added debt made possible by hedging allows a company to take advantage of the tax deductibility of interest payments.

Multinational companies must recognize that foreign-exchange risk affects not only cash flows but also investment opportunities. A number of complex issues arise with multinationals, but many of them can be illustrated with two examples. In each example, a company is planning to build a plant in Germany to manufacture cameras. In Example 1 it will sell the cameras in Germany, while in Example 2 it will sell them in the United States. In both cases, most of the company's cash flows come from its other businesses in the United States. How aggressively should it hedge the dollar/mark exchange rate?

Example 1. If the dollar depreciates relative to the mark, it will become more expensive (in dollar terms) to build the plant in Germany. But this does not mean that the company will want to build a smaller plant—or scrap the plant altogether—because the marks it receives from selling cameras in Germany will also be worth more in dollars. In other words, because the plant's costs and revenues are *both* mark-denominated, as long as the plant is economically attractive today, it will still be attractive if the dollar/mark rate changes. Therefore, just as Omega Drug wants to maintain its R&D despite the dollar's appreciation, this company would want to maintain its investment in Germany despite the dollar's depreciation. This calls for fairly aggressive hedging against a depreciation in the dollar to ensure that the company has enough marks to build the plant.

Example 2. The answer here is a bit more complex. Since the company is now manufacturing cameras for export back to the United States, a depreciation in the dollar makes it less attractive to manufacture in Germany. Dollar-denominated labor costs are simply higher when the mark is more valuable. Thus, any depreciation in the dollar raises the dollar cost of building the plant. But it also reduces the dollar income the company would receive from the plant. As a result, the company might want to scale back its investment or scrap the plant when the dollar depreciates. The value of investing falls, so there's less reason to hedge than in Example 1. This case is analogous to that of Omega Oil in that risk that hurts cash flows—namely, a depreciation of the dollar relative to the mark—also diminishes the appeal of investing. As a result, there is less reason to hedge the risk.

Of course, this assumes that the company hasn't yet committed to building the plant. If it has, then it would make sense to hedge the short-term risk of a dollar depreciation to ensure that the funds are available to continue the project. But if it hasn't committed, it is less important to hedge the longer-term risks.

Companies should pay close attention to the hedging strategies of their competitors. It is tempting for managers to think that if the competition doesn't hedge, then their company doesn't need to, either. However, there are some situations in which a company may have even greater reason to hedge if its competitors *don't*. Let's continue with the example of the camera company that is considering building capacity to manufacture and sell cameras in Germany. Suppose now that its competitors—other camera companies with revenues mostly in dollars—are also considering building capacity in Germany.

If its competitors choose not to hedge, they won't be in a strong position to add capacity if the dollar depreciates: they will find themselves short of marks. But that is precisely the situation in which the company *wants* to build its plant—when its competitors' weakness reduces the likelihood of industry overcapacity; this makes its investment in Germany more attractive. Therefore, the company should hedge to make sure it has enough cash for this investment.

This is just another example of how clearly articulating the nature of investment opportunities can inform a company's risk-management strategy; in this case, the investment opportunities depend on the overall structure of the industry and on the financial strength of its competitors. Thus, the same elements that go into formulating a competitive strategy should also be used to formulate a risk-management strategy.

The choice of specific derivatives cannot simply be delegated to the financial specialists in the company. It's true that many of the more technical aspects of derivatives trading are best left to the technical finance staff. But senior managers need to understand how the choices of financial instruments link up with the broader issues of risk-management strategy that we have been exploring.

There are two key features of derivatives that a company must keep in mind when evaluating which ones to use. The first is the cash-flow implications of the instruments. For example, futures contracts are traded on an exchange and require a company to mark to market on a daily basis—that is, to put up money to compensate for any short-term losses. These expenditures can cut into the cash a company needs to finance current investments. In contrast, over-the-counter forward contracts— which are customized transactions arranged with derivatives dealers—do not have this drawback because they do not have to be settled until the contract matures.

However, this advantage will probably come at some cost: when a dealer writes the company a forward, he will charge a premium for the risk that he bears by not extracting any payments until the contract matures.

The second feature of derivatives that should be kept in mind is the "linearity" or "nonlinearity" of the contracts. Futures and forwards are essentially linear contracts: for every dollar the company gains when the underlying variable moves in one direction by 10%, it loses a dollar when the underlying variable moves in the other direction by 10%. By contrast, options are nonlinear in that they allow the company to put a floor on its losses without having to give up the potential for gains. If there is a minimum amount of investment a company needs to maintain, options can allow it to lock in the necessary cash. At the same time, they provide the flexibility to increase investment in good times.

Again, the decision of which contract to use should be driven by the objective of aligning the demand for funds with the supply of internal funds. A skillful financial engineer may be good at pricing intricate financial contracts, but this alone does not indicate which types of contracts fit best with a company's risk-management strategy.

An important corollary to this point is that it probably makes good sense to stay away from the most exotic, customized hedging instruments unless there is a very clear investment-side justification for their use. Dealers make more profit selling cutting-edge instruments, for which competition is less intense. And each additional dollar of profit going to the dealer is a dollar less of value available to shareholders. So unless a company can explain why an exotic instrument protects its investment opportunities better than a plain-vanilla one, it's better to go with plain vanilla.

WHERE DO MANAGERS go from here? The first step—which may be the hardest—is to realize that they cannot ignore risk management. Some managers may be tempted to do so in order to avoid high-profile blunders like those of Procter & Gamble and Metallgesellschaft. But, as the Dresser Industries and Caterpillar examples show, this head-in-the-sand approach has costs as well. Nor can risk management simply be handed off to the financial staff. That approach can lead to poor coordination with overall corporate strategy and a patchwork of derivatives trades that may, when taken together, reduce overall corporate value. Instead, it's critical for a company to devise a risk-management strategy that is based on good investments and is aligned with its broader corporate objectives.

Demystifying Derivatives

AT FIRST GLANCE, the list of derivative products looks bewilderingly long. Forwards, futures, options, swaps, caps, and floors are just some of the more commonly used derivatives, and new ones are being designed all the time. However, all these products are derived from just two basic building blocks: forwards and options. Understanding how these two instruments work goes a long way toward demystifying derivatives.

Forward-Based Contracts: Forwards, Swaps, and Futures

Perhaps the most basic type of derivative is the forward contract. With a forward, the user promises to buy or sell an asset—say, oil, Treasury bills, or yen—at a specified price on a specified date. For example, a long forward position of 1,000 barrels of oil at a price of $20 per barrel, with a one-year maturity, obligates the user to buy 1,000 barrels of oil one year hence for $20,000. A short forward position obligates the user to deliver 1,000 barrels of oil (or its cash equivalent) for $20,000. Long positions enable hedgers to protect themselves against price increases in the underlying asset; short positions protect hedgers against price decreases.

Forward contracts have four important features:

Linearity. Forward contracts are linear: the gain when the value of the underlying asset moves in one direction is equal to the loss when the value of the asset moves by the same amount in the opposite direction. In the long forward position described above, the user makes a $1,000 profit when the oil price rises by $1 and loses $1,000 when it falls by $1.

No Money Down. When a forward contract is initiated, no money changes hands.

Settlement at Maturity. Forward contracts are not settled until their maturity date. In the case of the oil forward, no money changes hands for a year. While this feature may be convenient to hedgers, it comes with a price: there is a risk—known as "counterparty" risk—that the other party will be unable to meet its obligations on the maturity date.

Customization. Since forwards are privately arranged (traded over the counter) and not traded on an exchange, the terms of the forward—for example, the maturity date and the characteristics of the underlying asset—can be customized for the users.

Swaps are packages of forward contracts and share all the same basic features. They can be used to create hedges that extend over several time periods. A company that issues ten-year floating-rate debt requiring annual interest payments, for instance, can use a swap to convert its floating-rate liability to a fixed-rate obligation, thereby hedging against interest-rate increases. Such a swap is just a bundle of interest-rate forward contracts: one with a one-year maturity, another with a two-year maturity, and so on, up to ten years.

Futures contracts are also closely related to forwards. However, they are marked to market on a daily basis. In other words, cash is paid in by the user to cover any losses on the transaction, and it is paid out to the user to reflect any profits. The advantage of marking to market is that it greatly reduces counterparty risk. This feature enables futures to be traded anonymously on large exchanges, thereby generating both more liquidity and more competitive pricing.

Option-Based Contracts: Options, Caps, and Floors

The other building-block financial instrument is the option contract. It differs from a forward in that the holder of an option can choose to buy or sell the underlying asset at a specified price on a specified date but is not obligated to do so. For example, a call option on oil might grant the user the right to buy 1,000 barrels of oil at a price of $20 per barrel anytime between now and one year hence. Conversely, with a put option, the user would have the right to sell the oil at the agreed-upon price. Like long forward positions, call options protect hedgers against increases in the price of the underlying asset; like short forward positions, put options protect hedgers against price decreases.

Option-based contracts can be analyzed along the same four dimensions as forward-based contracts:

Nonlinearity. The fact that one is not obligated to exercise an option means that its payoffs are nonlinear, or asymmetrical, with respect to gains and losses. The holder of a call option on oil can profit a great deal if oil prices rise; if oil prices fall, however, the option is simply not exercised and the holder can walk away without taking any losses.

Money Down. Unlike forward-based contracts, options require an initial investment when the position is established. The user pays an option premium up front in exchange for the right to walk away later on.

Settlement at Exercise. While forwards are settled when they mature, options are settled when they are exercised, which may occur before the maturity date. They are typically not marked to market, so beyond the initial premium no further money changes hands until they are exercised.

Customization. Options are available both on exchanges and over the counter. The over-the-counter market offers greater opportunity for customization.

Caps and floors are to option contracts what swaps are to forward contracts: a cap is simply a package of call options, and a floor a package of put options. For example, if a company issues ten-year floating-rate debt that requires annual interest payments, it might simultaneously purchase a cap that ensures that its total interest costs do not exceed some target level. Such a cap would simply be a series of call options on the underlying interest rate.

Notes

1. The study, reported in *Derivatives: Practices and Principles*, was conducted by the Group of Thirty, an independent study group in Washington, D.C., made up of economists, bankers, and policymakers.

2. A more technical article on this subject, "Risk Management: Coordinating Corporate Investment and Financing Policies," was published by the authors in the *Journal of Finance*, vol. 48, 1993, p. 1629.

3. This view has been advanced in an influential series of papers by Stewart C. Myers of MIT's Sloan School of Management: "The Determinants of Corporate Borrowing," *Journal of Financial Economics*, vol. 4, 1977, p. 147; "Corporate Financing and Investment Decisions When Firms Have Information That Investors Do Not Have," coauthored with Nicholas Majluf, *Journal of Financial Economics*, vol. 13, 1984, p. 187; and "The Capital Structure Puzzle," *Journal of Finance*, vol. 39, 1984, p. 575.

4. See, for example, Jeffrey MacKie-Mason, "Do Firms Care Who Provides Their Financing?" in *Asymmetric*

Information, Corporate Finance, and Investment, ed. R. Glenn Hubbard (Chicago: University of Chicago Press, 1990), p. 63.

5. Paul Asquith and David Mullins, "Equity Issues and Offering Dilution," *Journal of Financial Economics*, vol. 15, 1986, p. 61.

6. See, for example, Steven Fazzari, R. Glenn Hubbard, and Bruce Petersen, "Financing Constraints and Corporate Investment," *Brookings Papers on Economic Activity*, no. 1, 1988, p. 141.

Originally published in November 1994
Reprint 94604

Disciplined Decisions

Aligning Strategy with the Financial Markets

MARTHA AMRAM AND NALIN KULATILAKA

Executive Summary

THE GOAL OF STRATEGY is clear—to increase shareholder value. But in volatile markets, it's difficult to predict how a particular investment will affect a company's value. Drawing on their own experiences and perspectives, managers come to different conclusions. It's hard to sort out whose answers are the right ones.

In fact, there is only one right answer—the answer of the financial markets. The markets are adept at calculating the value of an investment under uncertain conditions—exactly the challenge faced by business strategists. By applying the discipline of the markets, executives can avoid basing important decisions on subjective judgments about the future.

The application of market discipline to strategy involves three components. First, the decision is framed in terms of the real options it creates. Second, in evaluating an investment, all the relevant information on value and risk available in the financial markets is taken into account. Third, actual financial transactions are used, when appropriate, to acquire options or otherwise mitigate risk.

In a series of cases, the authors show how applying market discipline can help illuminate a range of common business decisions—whether to add production capacity, or to invest in a new venture, or to upgrade an information system, for example. By providing disciplined insight into the uncertainty present in all markets, the real-options approach lets executives think more clearly and realistically about complex and risky strategic decisions.

T HE GOAL OF STRATEGY IS CLEAR—to make investment decisions that lead to greater shareholder value. But when it comes to actually achieving that goal, things get fuzzy. In volatile markets, where prices and demand are always in flux, it's hard to predict how a particular investment will ultimately influence a company's value. Senior executives spend a lot of time structuring their decisions, tracing out possible implications, assigning probabilities, and assessing risk. Rarely, though, does everyone agree about how an investment will play out. Different managers draw on different experiences and have different perspectives, which lead them to different conclusions. It's hard to sort out whose answers are the right answers.

In fact, there is only one right answer: the answer of the financial markets. The markets are the final arbiter of an investment's value, and the markets are adept at calculating the impact of uncertainty on value. By applying the discipline of the markets, managers can avoid basing important decisions on subjective judgments about the future. They can incorporate the market's objective measures of value under uncertainty into their own strategic choices.

When does a decision become disciplined? Discipline, in our view, has three components:

- The decision is structured, or framed, in terms of the options it creates.

- All the relevant information on value and risk available in the financial markets is taken into account.

- Financial-market transactions are used to acquire options or otherwise mitigate risk whenever that's economically justified.

Applying market discipline changes the way managers make decisions, and it changes the decisions themselves. Consider the oil industry. Oil companies today place far more value on exploration than they did just a few years ago. They make higher bids for unexplored tracts, launch more exploration initiatives, and wait longer before abandoning an initiative. Why? Their investment decisions have become disciplined.

First, the oil companies now see that exploration creates options. If an exploration project is successful, a company has the option to drill wells and pump oil. If the project doesn't pan out, the company has the option to cease development and cut its losses. The options increase the value of the exploration project because they protect the full potential gain of the investment while reducing the possible losses.

Second, the oil companies draw on information from the financial markets to measure the value of the real options. An oil-field exploration project, after all, is very similar to a call-option contract on oil: both provide, for a specified cost, a right to get oil at some point down the road. The price of the financial option, therefore, says a lot about the value of the real option.

Third, oil companies buy and sell oil-related securities to further temper the price risks inherent in oil exploration. They know that sometimes it's cheaper to acquire a financial option than a real option.

All kinds of businesses have the opportunity to follow the oil companies' lead. By drawing on financial markets' techniques, benchmarks, and information, they can discipline their investment decisions and align them with the investment decisions of the markets. They can close the gap between strategy and shareholder value.

Uncovering Real Options

Taking an options-based approach is not simply a matter of using a new set of valuation equations and models. It requires a new way of framing strategic decisions. The question becomes less, What will we gain by moving from point A to point B? and more, If we begin down the path from point A to point B, what options will open for us and what will we gain by having those options? The first step in reorienting strategic thinking, then, is to identify the real options that exist in investment decisions.

Uncovering real options can be tough. Unlike financial options, real options are not precisely defined or neatly packaged. But they do exist in almost every business decision, and they tend to take a limited number of forms. By understanding these forms, managers can become better able to spot the options in their own decisions. The following are hypothetical examples of the most common types of real options.

TIMING OPTIONS

Sales of low-fat ice cream are surging. Operating at full capacity, the Healthy Cow Creamery is considering whether to expand its plant. Launching the expansion would require a big up-front investment, and the company's managers can't be sure that the sales boom will persist. They have the option of delaying the investment until they learn more about the strength of demand. It may be that the risk avoided by waiting to invest has a greater value than the sales that might be forfeited by postponing construction.

GROWTH OPTIONS

Friend-to-Friend, a company that sells cosmetics through a network of independent salespeople, is trying to decide whether to enter the vast Chinese market. The initial investment to build a manufacturing and sales organization would be large, but it may lead to the opportunity to sell a whole range of products through an established sales network. The investment would thus create growth options that have value above and beyond the returns generated by the initial operation.

STAGING OPTIONS

The top management team at International Widget is reviewing a proposal from the senior vice president of operations to install a new manufacturing system. The proposal calls for a full, multimillion-dollar rollout at all factories over the next two years. But the business benefits of the project remain uncertain. The company has the option to invest in the new system in stages rather than all at once. The conclusion of each stage will in turn provide further options—for continuing, for delaying, or for abandoning the effort. All these options add value to the proposed project.

EXIT OPTIONS

Molecular Sciences has a patent for a promising new chemical product, but it's worried about the size of the market opportunity, and it's unsure whether the manufacturing process will meet government regulations regarding toxic chemicals. If the company does begin an effort to commercialize the product, though, it will still have the option to abandon the project if demand doesn't materialize or if the environmental liability appears too large. The exit option increases the value of the project because it reduces the size of the investment at risk.

FLEXIBILITY OPTIONS

Cell, Incorporated needs to decide how best to manufacture its latest cellular telephone. Demand for the new product is uncertain, although forecasts indicate that sales will be spread across two continents. A traditional manufacturing analysis indicates that a single plant would be much cheaper to build and operate than two plants on two continents. But the analysis fails to take into account the flexibility option that would be created by building two plants—the option to shift production from continent to continent in response to shifts in demand, exchange rates, or production costs. If the value of the option outweighs the cost saved by building just one plant, then Cell should invest in two plants and carry the excess capacity.

OPERATING OPTIONS

Bright Light Software has long contracted with other companies to produce and package its CD-ROMs. Its sales have grown rapidly in recent years, however, and now the company is trying to decide whether it makes economic sense to build its own plant. If it goes ahead, it would gain a number of operating options. It would, for example, have the option to shut down the operation during times of weak demand and the option to run additional shifts during times of high demand. The value of these options adds to the value of the plant.

LEARNING OPTIONS

Hollywood Partners is planning to release three movies in the midst of the Christmas season. Before the films actually open, the studio's executives can't tell which one will be the biggest hit, so they can't be sure how best to allocate their marketing and advertising dollars. But they have an important learning option. They can release each movie on a limited number of screens in selected cities and then refine their marketing plans based on what they learn. They can, for example, roll out the most popular movie nationwide and give it a large advertising budget while putting the other films into more limited release.

This list is illustrative, but it does not reflect the way options actually occur in the real world. An option rarely arises in isolation. It usually comes as part of a complex bundle. In deciding to build a new plant, for example, a company will need to weigh the value of the initial timing and staging options, but it will also need to look ahead to the growth, operating, and exit options that the plant would create. Moreover, one option can take different forms. An operating option, for example, may lead to increased revenues and thus might also be viewed as a growth option. Much of the challenge in taking an options approach to strategy lies in identifying the full set of options you have, disentangling them from one another, and deciding which are the most valuable.

Once you've framed your decision in terms of real options, you can look to the markets to gather the information you need to evaluate those options. In thinking about how to apply information from financial markets to a complicated strategic decision, we find that it's useful to think in terms of the decision's *distance from the market*. Some decisions seem very near to the market— there's a clear and tight link between the real options and existing financial securities. Oil companies, for example, have no problem seeing how the value of oil option contracts mirrors the value of their own exploration options. Other decisions seem far removed from the market—the available financial options are not clearly analogous to the real options. Executives at some companies might assume that because their decisions seem distant from the markets, they won't be able to learn much from a real-options approach. But, in fact, as more and more risks are becoming securitized, the real-options frontier is steadily expanding. Today, the financial markets can help illuminate most strategic decisions.

Applying the Discipline

Let's look at how three very different kinds of decisions can be disciplined by the financial markets by looking at three hypothetical examples. We'll start with a situation that is relatively close to the markets: building a manufacturing plant whose raw-materials and products are both traded in the futures market. The second situation we'll look at is a bit more distant from the markets: launching a startup company that is similar to other publicly traded companies. Finally, we'll examine what may seem like the quintessential internally focused investment, one that seemingly would have little to do with markets: upgrading an information system. We'll show that, even when a decision appears to be distant from the financial markets, it can be disciplined by the markets. (See the exhibit "The Real-Options Frontier.")

SHOULD WE BUILD A NEW PLANT?

Chicago Soy Processing has long-term fixed-price contracts to buy crops from several farmers. Each year, it knows the price it will pay for beans but not the quantity it will have to buy. Judging by the weather, this year's harvest looks like it will be a bumper crop, and it is likely that Chicago Soy will have to take delivery on an unusually large volume of beans. The company needs to decide whether to build a new plant to process the beans or to reserve capacity from another processor.

As Chicago Soy's managers begin to think through the decision, they realize that building a new processing plant would create a number of operating options. One of the most valuable would be the option to shut down the plant temporarily—and thus save considerable operating costs—during times of low supply. The shutdown, or mothballing, option has value because it mitigates risk, providing Chicago Soy with flexibility as it responds to the uncertainties of its business. To accurately gauge

---

The Real-Options Frontier

How applicable is real-options thinking to a particular business decision? That depends on the decision's complexity and its distance from the markets. Valuations of simple decisions that are close to the markets—that is, where there are close parallels between the real options and existing financial options—can often be done using standard option-pricing formulas such as the Black-Scholes equation. As complexity and distance increase, customized valuation models become necessary. At some point— which we call the real-options frontier—decisions become so complex and so distant that valuation becomes impracticable with existing tools.

In this exhibit, we plot the three cases examined in this article according to their complexity and distance. Chicago Soy's decision is close to the financial markets—it involves routinely traded commodities—and it is relatively simple, so the valuation of the options requires a fairly straightforward model. The decisions faced by Portlandia Ale and, in particular, Eastern States Mortgage are much further from the market; they require more highly customized models.

The frontier of the real-options approach continues to expand outward as new markets emerge. Many real options that would have been impossible to value objectively a few years ago can now be valued with a high degree of discipline.

the overall value of the plant, the company needs to account for the value of the mothballing option as well as the value of the other options it will gain.

By looking to the financial markets, Chicago Soy can gather information it will need to think through the value of its options and arrive at the best decision. The difference between the spot price of soybeans and the spot price of soybean oil—what's called the *crush spread*—tells a lot, for example, about the market value of processing capacity.

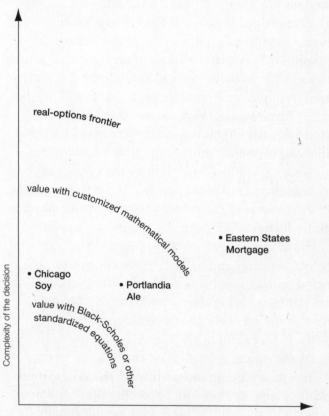

When the spread is large, less-efficient plants are drawn into the market, but when the spread narrows, the less-efficient plants become unprofitable and are shut down. The crush spread, in other words, reflects the efficiency of the least-efficient active processor.

In addition to the spot market, there's also a futures market not only for the beans and the oil but also for the crush spread. The prices of those contracts constitute the market's forecast of the path prices will take in the future. By looking at the prices of crush-spread futures, the company can see if it would be able to process the beans efficiently at the time of the harvest. Even more important, it gains insight into the longer-term value of the new plant. Looking at a range of crush-spread futures for a succession of delivery dates can tell the company what levels of processing efficiency its plant will need in order to be profitable at various points in the future. Chicago Soy can use this information to project when it would make economic and competitive sense to shut down its new plant and to determine the impact of those shutdowns on overall plant profitability. It thus gains an objective measure of the value of the mothballing option.

But that's not all. Because it costs money to shut down and reopen a plant, mothballing decisions should not be made purely on the basis of the current or projected crush spread. By examining the volatility of the futures contracts for crush spreads, the company can glean information about the uncertainty of the price forecasts. If, for example, the spread is highly volatile, the company may want to hold off on shutting down its plant even when the spread narrows to the point where the plant is unprofitable. The possibility that the spread may soon widen—and the plant may again become profitable—argues for a delay in incurring the shutdown costs. By looking at the volatility of the crush spread, Chicago Soy thus gains an even more accurate sense of the value of its mothballing option and of the new plant in general.

The information drawn from the financial markets is not just useful for evaluating investments and plotting strategy. It can also be applied to tactical operating decisions. Chicago Soy's analysis of the crush spread and its volatility, for example, revealed objective trigger points for shutting down and reopening its processing plants. In making such operating decisions, the company can now take into account not only the current and expected future prices of beans and oil but also the volatility of those prices. Because the trigger points are derived from traded securities, they align the plant's operations with the markets, ensuring that it operates in a way that maximizes shareholder value.

If it turns out that an investment in a new plant is not economically justified, market information can help Chicago Soy think in a disciplined way about its options for reserving capacity at another processor. Looking at the crush-spread futures, it can infer a market price for the capacity at the time Chicago Soy will require it, thus giving the company an objective benchmark for evaluating the terms of any contract it may be offered. Depending on what it learns from the markets, Chicago Soy might want to explore various contractual alternatives. It may, for example, want to make a commitment to take the reserved capacity regardless of the size of the harvest. Or it may want to negotiate an option on the capacity, paying a small amount now for the opportunity to preserve flexibility at harvest time. It may also decide to shift some of its risk by selling futures contracts on the beans it will receive.

Now think about how Chicago Soy would operate without a disciplined decision process. First, it would develop private forecasts of prices, ignoring the information in the market securities. Second, it would overlook the value of the operating options the new plant would provide, leading it to underestimate the value of investing in additional capacity. Third, it would develop some scenarios about the harvest—big crop, medium crop, small crop—and then assign subjective probabilities to them. Such scenarios would highlight the value of flexibility, but they could also lead to subjective trigger points. The company might keep a plant open too long, operating when the crush spread is too narrow to turn a profit. Or it might keep a plant closed too long, forgoing profits. Finally, traditional analyses tend to focus solely on physical capacity, overlooking the potential for acquiring options through contracts. Market discipline requires that a contractual option be used whenever it's cheaper than an identical real option.

SHOULD WE LAUNCH A NEW COMPANY?

Portlandia Ale exists only as the dream of two young brew masters who yearn to go into business for themselves. To make their dream a reality, the two will need $4 million immediately to begin product development and manufacturing, another $12 million in two years for the marketing effort required to launch the products, and a final $3 million in three years to complete a distribution system. The entrepreneurs are very optimistic, despite considerable uncertainty about the value of the market opportunity they're chasing. The key question facing them, and their potential investors, is this: Is Portlandia Ale a viable business opportunity?

A traditional valuation analysis would seek a single precise answer. One can easily imagine the spreadsheet that would be used. The first row would show steadily growing revenues; the second row would display gross profits. Lower down would be a row with the planned investments—a few cells containing large negative cash flows. The net cash flow would be calculated along the bottom row. In the bottom right-hand corner, where the forecasts of net cash flows end, would appear the final entry: the net cash flow at the end of the forecast period multiplied by the average price-earnings ratio for microbrewers. This figure, known as the terminal value, represents the value of the continuing business after the last year shown on the spreadsheet. The value of the proposed microbrewery would then be calculated as the present value of the forecasted stream of net cash flows. The traditional analysis would conclude that Portlandia is a viable opportunity if its present value is positive.

What's wrong with this analysis? First, the real world is uncertain. Any forecast is but one of many possible outcomes. Second, traditional analyses tend to build a positive outcome into the calculations. Typically, projected cash flows become positive only toward the end of the forecast period, at which point they're translated into a terminal value. That means a positive net present value is usually based on only a short period of profitable operations and a terminal value whose magnitude is suspect. It is not uncommon for terminal values to contribute 85% or more of the total value in a standard analysis of a new business opportunity. Because the terminal value is so easy to manipulate, traditional business valuations are fundamentally undisciplined and fundamentally unreliable. (See the exhibit "The Flaw in Traditional Valuation Approaches.")

A better way to approach the valuation is to look at the opportunity as a succession of growth options. The initial $4 million investment buys the brew masters and their investors an option to make the $12 million and $3 million follow-on investments. But it does not obligate them to make those investments. If the microbrewery's prospects look unfavorable in two years' time, they can choose not to exercise the option and simply walk away. In making a valuation, then, the right question to ask is not What return will we gain from our investment in this company? But how valuable are the growth options that would be created by each successive investment in the new company? Answering that question leads naturally to the answer to the key strategic question: What growth strategy will create the greatest value?

The Flaw in Traditional Valuation Approaches

Deciding whether or not to pursue a new business opportunity requires an estimate of what the business will ultimately be worth. Traditional valuation tools use forecasts of outcomes (sales, profits, and so on) of future investments and of terminal values to arrive at seemingly precise numbers. But that imposes a fixed path on a business's future development.

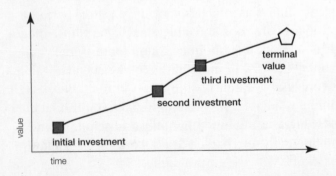

As managers well know, the fixed path view is artificial. In reality, pursuing a new business opportunity may result in a variety of outcomes that call for a wide range of strategic responses. We call that range the cone of uncertainty:

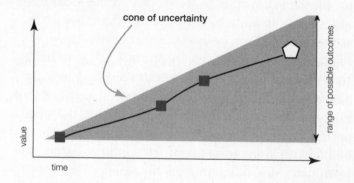

The real-options approach recognizes this uncertainty. It sees what managers see: that an investment today creates opportunities, or options, to change operating and investment decisions later depending on the actual outcome. Those future decisions will be contingent on the way events unfold:

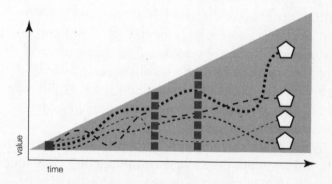

By identifying and determining the value of growth options, managers will gain a more accurate assessment of the wisdom of an initial investment.

The growth options have value because the future is uncertain. We don't know whether Portlandia will go bust or turn into the next Sam Adams. By buying the initial option, the investors gain access to the potential upside while limiting the losses they would incur from unfavorable outcomes. In two years, when they arrive at the next decision point—the next option-buying opportunity—some of the uncertainty will have been resolved, and they will be in a better position to make a new investment choice. If Portlandia is struggling, they may want to hold off on further investment. If it's had a particularly propitious start, they may want to accelerate and make a larger investment. The options-based approach to valuation mirrors the reality of management: every investment decision you make changes the set of investments you can make in the future.

The value of the growth options is calculated by first determining the value of the mature business (once all options have been exercised) and then measuring the uncertainty of actually realizing that value. Both can be derived from market information. The value of the mature business can be based on stock-market ratios— such as price-to-sales and price-to-cash-flow figures—for existing mature microbreweries. And the measure of uncertainty can be based on the historical volatility of microbrewery stocks. Once you know the volatility, standard option-pricing formulas can be adapted to determine the option values.

As the Portlandia example demonstrates, the growth-option framework works well for valuing new companies in established markets where the stock prices of existing companies provide benchmarks. But is the approach applicable in new markets? The answer is usually yes, although the approach will vary slightly depending on whether the new market operates according to established business models or according to new, evolving models.

Kendall Square Research in Waltham, Massachusetts, is an example of the first situation. The company was the first maker of massively-parallel-processing computers to go public. But while its product was entirely new, its business model closely followed that of other big-computer makers. The valuation of Kendall Square's initial public offering could thus be made in a disciplined manner by drawing on the market valuations of those similar companies.

Netscape is an example of the other situation. When it became the first Web-browser company to go public, the entire Internet industry was in its infancy, and Netscape's business model was evolving rapidly and unpredictably. There were no similar companies. But even though the links to market discipline were weaker, they were not nonexistent. Netscape's potential range of outcomes could be estimated by examining the volatility of a stock index of newly public companies in the technology sector.

SHOULD WE UPGRADE OUR INFORMATION SYSTEM?

The senior executives of Eastern States Mortgage were trying to decide whether to accept the chief information officer's proposal for a major IT upgrade. The CIO argued that an enhanced system, with state-of-the-art image-processing capabilities, would enable Eastern States to significantly improve its customer service, leading to stronger growth. The upgrade, as proposed, would require large up-front expenditures and changes in the company's operating practices. But according to the proposal's projections, the initial costs would be far outweighed by higher mortgage sales over the long run. The CIO estimated the upgrade's net present value at $500,000.

At first glance, a decision about an IT upgrade would seem to have little to do with the financial markets. The big risks all appear to be unique to the company. They're what we call *private risk*. Will the company be able to bring in the system on budget and on time? Will its people be able to change the way they do business? Will the new image-processing capabilities really make a difference in how customers perceive their service? In fact, however, Eastern States' management team found that market discipline could help in both structuring and evaluating their decision.

An enhancement to an information system, like any improvement to a business's infrastructure, creates options by providing a platform for future upgrades and extensions. With better information-processing capabilities, Eastern States would gain new growth options and new operating options. It could, for instance, begin to customize its mortgage packages to the needs of individual customers, providing opportunities to further increase demand. And it would be in a position to reduce its costs by more efficiently delivering mortgage pools to the financial markets.

When the managers began to think in terms of options, they saw that the investment in an upgraded system should be considered not as a single up-front cost but rather as a series of investments made in stages. The conclusion of each stage would provide a new set of options for continuing, revising, or abandoning the initiative.

To be able to explicitly evaluate all the options, the managers structured the proposed upgrade into three stages. The initial stage consisted of a pilot project conducted in one region. The pilot project would show management whether or not the new technology could be implemented and used successfully by the company. It would, in other words, resolve many of the private risks. At that point, the risk in the project would actually become dominated not by private risk but by a market-priced risk—in this case, the risk that interest rates might rise to a level that would dampen overall mortgage demand. The size of that risk hinged on the volatility of interest rates, which could be measured in a disciplined way by using an index of interestrate securities tailored to reflect the maturities and features of the mortgages Eastern States sold.

If the pilot was successful and the interest-rate risk within acceptable limits, the company would move on to stage two: rolling out the technology on the retail side of the business. At the end of that stage, a disciplined decision about risk would again be made before making the final investment to roll out the upgraded system to the rest of the company. The successful conclusion of the third stage would, in turn, open new options for the company. Eastern States would, for example, have the option of making a further investment in systems that could create customized mortgages. That option could be evaluated in a similarly disciplined manner.

Using traditional valuation tools and assuming that all three stages of the investment would necessarily be completed, the CIO had estimated the net present value of the imaging upgrade at $500,000. Senior managers then revised the CIO's overly optimistic forecasts and arrived at an NPV of negative $380,000—clearly indicating that the project was not worth pursuing.

But reframing the choice to account for options resulted in a very different answer. When the value of the options inherent in the project was taken into account, the NPV of the investment rose to $2.1 million. Most of the increase came from two sources: the value of being able to reduce the downside risk (by ceasing further investment at the end of each stage) and the value of the potential for a strong upside gain (if the technology worked and interest rates dropped). The company launched the pilot project.

In addition to changing the outcome of this particular decision, the real-options approach fundamentally changed the way management thought about information technology. Eastern States, like many companies, had struggled with IT investments in the past. It had been unable to tie proposed investments to business goals, and as a result decisions to spend large sums of money were made—or not made—based on emotion, charisma, or sheer exhaustion. By explicitly laying out the real options created by an IT investment, the company was able to move from subjective to objective analysis, from undisciplined to disciplined thinking. It could assess each stage of a potential investment on the basis of whether it would further the company's business objectives and pay off under actual market conditions. The criteria for each successive investment decision were clear, providing the managers with a rational review process.

Rethinking Strategy

The three cases we've looked at illustrate the broad applicability of a disciplined, real-options approach.

Companies routinely have to make tough choices about capacity, just as Chicago Soy did. They can discipline their decisions by identifying and evaluating their operating options. Companies routinely have to estimate the value of a new business or product, just as Portlandia Ale did. They can discipline their decisions by focusing on the value of their growth options. And companies routinely have to make hard decisions about infrastructure investments, just as Eastern States Mortgage did. They can discipline their decisions by looking at the options created at each stage of the prospective investment. No company's investment decisions are wholly isolated from the financial markets.

That doesn't mean that every decision can be completely illuminated by market discipline. Nor does it mean that achieving discipline is easy. Because real options are complex and generally involve private as well as market-priced risk, their value usually cannot be measured as precisely as that of financial options. Knowing the limits of the real-options approach is an important part of using the approach successfully. (See the insert "The Limits of Discipline.")

The good news is that the rapid pace of financial innovation will continue to expand the applicability and reliability of real-options thinking. Option valuation tools and models are constantly being improved, and additional types of risk are constantly being securitized. Many risks that once had to be considered private risks have turned into market-priced risks. The recent introduction of catastrophe bonds, for example, gives companies an objective benchmark for evaluating how much to invest to mitigate the risk of an earthquake, either by strengthening a building or by buying insurance. And the establishment of a trading market for sulfur dioxide emissions has enabled manufacturers and energy companies to think systematically about the most economic way to reduce pollution.

So why haven't more companies adopted the real-options approach to making strategic decisions? We believe that the approach has been slow to spread to the business world because much of the discussion about it has centered on arcane equations and models. The complexity of the tools has obscured the power of the underlying idea. The real value of real options, we believe, lies not in the outputs of Black-Scholes or other formulas but in the reshaping of executives' thinking about strategic investment. By providing objective insight into the uncertainty present in all markets, the real-options approach enables executives to think more clearly and more realistically about complex and risky strategy decisions. It brings strategy and shareholder value into harmony.

The Limits of Discipline

TOOLS FOR VALUING options have existed for only about 30 years, and the concept of real options is newer still. It should come as no surprise, therefore, that determining the value of real options remains an inexact science. The application of market discipline has its limits, which need to be carefully considered in making any decision.

Because of these limitations, the actual answers you get from a real-options approach to valuation can diverge from the theoretical best answers. We would argue, though, that even with these distortions, the real-options approach will lead to better decisions than traditional approaches produce. Moreover, the frontier of the real-options approach continues to advance rapidly. The models are becoming more sophisticated, and the information from the markets is becoming more robust. The limits, in turn, grow fewer.

- **Model risk.** Once a financial-option contract is written, or once a real option is identified, a valuation model must be created. But sometimes there is not enough objective information in the financial markets to get the model's mathematics exactly right. The difference between the model's answers and the theoretically correct answers represents the model risk. For simple or short-term financial contracts, little model risk will exist. But for complex options, and long-lived contracts, the model may be quite far from the way events actually turn out. As a result, the company will bear greater risk than it anticipated. As traders and managers become more experienced with options, they will become better able to anticipate and allow for modeling errors. In the meantime, managers need to be aware of model risk and take it into account when using model outputs.

- **Imperfect proxies.** Let's say you want to write a contract based on the price of natural gas in St. Louis in December, but the only natural-gas future currently traded is based on delivery in New York. If gas prices in December are different in St. Louis than they are in New York, you've got an imperfect proxy. How imperfect the proxy is and how important it is to your business will determine the severity of the impact. If the impact promises to

be large, it may be possible to get an investment
bank or a commodity dealer to create a tailored
contract for you.

- **Lack of observable prices.** Sometimes, price data
are not available from the market as quickly as you
need them to make strategic decisions. The relevant
securities may not be traded very frequently, for
example, or reports on the trades may be delayed.
Without hard data, you may need to rely on
educated guesses about price movements when
making decisions about whether to buy, sell, or
exercise an option. Guessing will increase the
possibility that you will not realize an option's
full value. The fast diffusion of electronic trading
systems is reducing this problem by accelerating
the dissemination of price data.

- **Lack of liquidity.** Real assets and thinly traded
stocks tend to share a common problem: a lack of
liquidity. The trading volume is so low that any siz-
able trade can move the price. If, for example, you
decide to exercise an option to abandon an asset,
your intention to sell can move the price of the
asset down further. Again, you won't capture the
full value of the option as modeled. Traders in
financial markets have adopted various trading
techniques to mitigate the distortions caused by a
lack of liquidity, and some of them can be adopted
by the users of real options.

- **Private risk.** The value of many real options is heavily influenced by private risk—risk that is peculiar to
one company. Private risk takes many forms, ranging from the possibility that an advertising campaign will fail to the potential that a company's

employees will lack the skills necessary to carry out a particular initiative. Because managers are used to thinking about private risk, they tend to give it too much emphasis when they make strategic decisions. It overwhelms their models. A better approach is to consider only the most important sources of private risk and to ensure that they're in balance with the key sources of market-priced risk.

Originally published in January 1999
Reprint 99101

Six Rules for Effective Forecasting

PAUL SAFFO

Executive Summary

THE PRIMARY GOAL OF FORECASTING is to
identify the full range of possibilities facing a company, society, or the world at large. In this article,
Saffo demythologizes the forecasting process to
help executives become sophisticated and participative consumers of forecasts, rather than passive
absorbers. He illustrates how to use forecasts to at
once broaden understanding of possibilities and
narrow the decision space within which one must
exercise intuition.

The events of 9/11, for example, were a much
bigger surprise than they should have been. After
all, airliners flown into monuments were the stuff of
Tom Clancy novels in the 1990s, and everyone
knew that terrorists had a very personal antipathy
toward the World Trade Center. So why was

9/11 such a surprise? What can executives do
to avoid being blindsided by other such wild
cards, be they radical shifts in markets or the
seemingly sudden emergence of disruptive
technologies?

In describing what forecasters are trying to
achieve. Saffo outlines six simple, commonsense
rules that smart managers should observe as they
embark on a voyage of discovery with professional
forecasters. Map a cone of uncertainty, he advises,
look for the S curve, embrace the things that don't
fit, hold strong opinions weakly, look back twice
as far as you look forward, and know when *not*
to make a forecast.

PEOPLE AT COCKTAIL PARTIES are always asking
me for stock tips, and then they want to know how my
predictions have turned out. Their requests reveal the
common but fundamentally erroneous perception that
forecasters make predictions. We don't, of course: Prediction is possible only in a world in which events are
preordained and no amount of action in the present can
influence future outcomes. That world is the stuff of
myth and superstition. The one we inhabit is quite different—little is certain, nothing is preordained, and what
we do in the present affects how events unfold, often in
significant, unexpected ways.

The role of the forecaster in the real world is quite different from that of the mythical seer. Prediction is concerned with future certainty; forecasting looks at how
hidden currents in the present signal possible changes in
direction for companies, societies, or the world at large.

Thus, the primary goal of forecasting is to identify the full range of possibilities, not a limited set of illusory certainties. Whether a specific forecast actually turns out to be accurate is only part of the picture—even a broken clock is right twice a day. Above all, the forecaster's task is to map uncertainty, for in a world where our actions in the present influence the future, uncertainty is opportunity.

Unlike a prediction, a forecast must have a logic to it. That's what lifts forecasting out of the dark realm of superstition. The forecaster must be able to articulate and defend that logic. Moreover, the consumer of the forecast must understand enough of the forecast process and logic to make an independent assessment of its quality—and to properly account for the opportunities and risks it presents. The wise consumer of a forecast is not a trusting bystander but a participant and, above all, a critic.

Even after you have sorted out your forecasters from the seers and prophets, you still face the task of distinguishing good forecasts from bad, and that's where this article comes in. In the following pages, I try to demythologize the forecasting process so that you can become a more sophisticated and participative consumer of forecasts, rather than a passive absorber. I offer a set of simple, commonsense rules that you can use as you embark on a voyage of discovery with professional forecasters. Most important, I hope to give you the tools to evaluate forecasts for yourself.

Rule 1: Define a Cone of Uncertainty

As a decision maker, you ultimately have to rely on your intuition and judgment. There's no getting around that in a world of uncertainty. But effective forecasting provides essential context that informs your intuition. It broadens your understanding by revealing overlooked possibilities and exposing unexamined assumptions regarding hoped-for outcomes. At the same time, it narrows the decision space within which you must exercise your intuition.

I visualize this process as mapping a *cone of uncertainty*, a tool I use to delineate possibilities that extend out from a particular moment or event. The forecaster's job is to define the cone in a manner that helps the decision maker exercise strategic judgment. Many factors go into delineating the cone of uncertainty, but the most important is defining its breadth, which is a measure of overall uncertainty. Other factors—relationships among elements, for example, and the ranking of possible outcomes—must also be considered in developing a forecast, but determining the cone's breadth is the crucial first step. Imagine it is 1997, the Toyota Prius has just gone on sale in Japan, and you are forecasting the future of the market for hybrid cars in the United States. External factors to consider would be oil price trends and consumer attitudes regarding the environment, as well as more general factors such as economic trends. Inside the cone would be factors such as the possible emergence of competing technologies (for instance, fuel cells) and an increased consumer preference for small cars (such as the Mini). At the edge of the cone would be wild cards like a terrorist attack or a war in the Middle East. These are just a very few representative examples. (See the exhibit "Mapping the Cone of Uncertainty" for more on the process.)

Drawing a cone too narrowly is worse than drawing it too broadly. A broad cone leaves you with a lot of uncertainty, but uncertainty is a friend, for its bedfellow is

Mapping the Cone of Uncertainty

A cone of uncertainty delineates the possibilities that extend out from a particular moment or event. The most important factor in mapping a cone is defining its breadth, which is a measure of overall uncertainty. In other words, the forecaster determines what range of events or products the cone should encompass. Drawing the cone is a dynamic process, and what we see here is just one iteration.

Let's take the case of robot products, a minicraze that has been emerging and subsiding since the mid-1980s. The events before 2007 indicate that activity in this area is building, and it seems only a matter of time before this industry takes off, in the same way PCs took off in the mid-1980s and the Web took off in the mid-1990s.

In drawing this cone, my first step was to note the distinction between appliance-centric robots and entertainment-centric robots, represented by the dotted line across the middle of the cone. The closer to the dotted line a particular product or event is, the more it has in common with the category on the opposite side of the line. The DARPA Grand Challenges, which may end up as the indicators of robotic highway vehicles, are military projects and are thus located far from the dotted line in the middle of the cone.

In the neck of the cone is a key speculation: Who will be the entrepreneur who launches the robot craze? Deeper in the cone are several possible outcomes; the closer to the center of the cone's main axis they are, the more likely these events are to transpire. Along the edges of the cone are less likely events—the wild cards—which, if they did happen, would be transformative (like the emergence of intelligent robot companions).

Note that I've left plenty of blank spaces—this is where I will add to or refine my forecast. Above all, forecasts are meant to be scribbled on, disagreed with, and tossed out—and replaced with new, better ones.

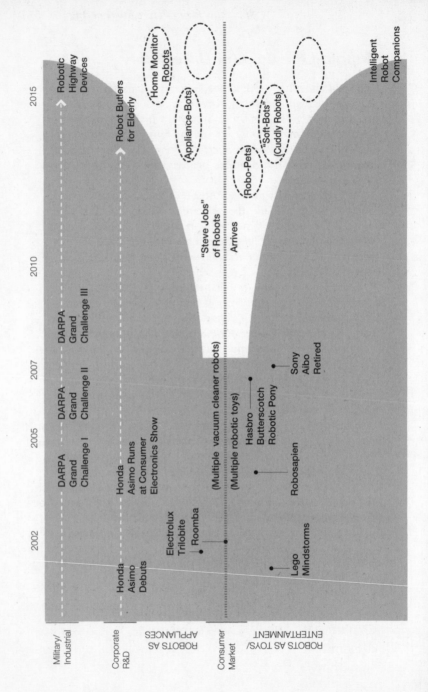

opportunity—as any good underwriter knows. The cone can be narrowed in subsequent refinements. Indeed, good forecasting is always an iterative process. Defining the cone broadly at the start maximizes your capacity to generate hypotheses about outcomes and eventual responses. A cone that is too narrow, by contrast, leaves you open to avoidable unpleasant surprises. Worse, it may cause you to miss the most important opportunities on your horizon.

The art of defining the cone's edge lies in carefully distinguishing between the highly improbable and the wildly impossible. Outliers—variously, wild cards or surprises—are what define this edge. A good boundary is one made up of elements lying on the ragged edge of plausibility. They are outcomes that might conceivably happen but make one uncomfortable even to contemplate.

The most commonly considered outliers are wild cards. These are trends or events that have low probabilities of occurrence (under 10%) or probabilities you simply cannot quantify but that, if the events were to occur, would have a disproportionately large impact. My favorite example of a wild card, because its probability is so uncertain and its impact so great, is finding radio evidence of intelligent life somewhere else in the universe. Nobody knows if we will ever receive a message (radio astronomers have been listening since the late 1950s), but if we did, it would send a vast and unpredictable tremor through the zeitgeist. One-third of the world's population would probably worship the remote intelligences, one-third would want to conquer them, and the final third (the readers of this magazine) would want to do some extraterrestrial market research and sell them something.

The tricky part about wild cards is that it is difficult to acknowledge sufficiently outlandish possibilities without losing your audience. The problem—and the essence of what makes forecasting hard—is that human nature is hardwired to abhor uncertainty. We are fascinated by change, but in our effort to avoid uncertainty we either dismiss outliers entirely or attempt to turn them into certainties that they are not. This is what happened with the Y2K problem in the final years before January 1, 2000. Opinions clustered at the extremes, with one group dismissing the predictions of calamity and another stocking up on survival supplies. The correct posture toward Y2K was that it was a wild card—an event with high potential impact but very low likelihood of occurrence, thanks to years of hard work by legions of programmers fixing old code.

The result of the Y2K nonevent was that many people concluded they had been the victims of someone crying Y2K wolf, and they subsequently rejected the possibility of other wild cards ever coming to pass. Consideration of anything unlikely became unfashionable, and as a result, 9/11 was a much bigger surprise than it should have been. After all, airliners flown into monuments were the stuff of Tom Clancy novels in the 1990s (inspired by Clancy, I helped write a scenario for the U.S. Air Force in 1997 that opened with a plane being flown into the Pentagon), and it was widely known that the terrorists had a very personal antipathy toward the World Trade Center. Yet the few people who took this wild card seriously were all but dismissed by those who should have been paying close attention.

Human nature being what it is, we are just as likely to overreact to an unexpected wild card by seeing new wild cards everywhere. That's a danger because it can lead you to draw a hollow cone—one that is cluttered with distracting outliers at the edge and neglected probabilities at the center. So don't focus on the edge to the exclusion of the center, or you will be surprised by an overlooked certainty. Above all, ask hard questions about whether a seeming wild card in fact deserves to be moved closer to the center.

Rule 2: Look for the S Curve

Change rarely unfolds in a straight line. The most important developments typically follow the S-curve shape of a power law: Change starts slowly and incrementally, putters along quietly, and then suddenly explodes, eventually tapering off and even dropping back down.

The mother of all S curves of the past 50 years is the curve of Moore's Law, the name given to Gordon Moore's brilliant 1965 conjecture that the density of circuits on a silicon wafer doubles every 18 months. We can all feel the consequences of Moore's Law in the extravagant surprises served up by the digital revolution swirling around us. Of course, the curve of Moore's Law is still unfolding—it is still a "J"—with the top of the "S" nowhere in sight. But it will flatten eventually, certainly with regard to silicon circuit density. Even here, though, engineers are sure to substitute denser circuit-carrying materials (like nanoscale and biological materials) as each successive material reaches saturation, so the broadest form of the Moore's Law curve (density regardless of the material) will keep climbing for some time to come. This distinction reveals another important feature of S curves, which is that they are fractal in nature. Very large, broadly defined curves are composed of small, precisely defined and linked S curves. For a forecaster, the discovery of an emergent S curve should lead you to suspect a larger, more important curve lurking in the background. Miss the larger curve and your strategy may amount to standing on a whale, fishing for minnows.

The art of forecasting is to identify an S-curve pattern as it begins to emerge, well ahead of the inflection point. The tricky part of S curves is that they inevitably invite us to focus on the inflection point, that dramatic moment of takeoff when fortunes are made and revolutions launched. But the wise forecaster will look to the left of the curve in hopes of identifying the inflection point's inevitable precursors. Consider Columbus's 1492 voyage. His discovery falls at the inflection point of Western exploration. Columbus was not the first fifteenth-century explorer to go to the New World—he was the first to make it back, and he did so at a moment when his discovery would land like a spark in the economic tinder of a newly emergent Europe and launch thousands upon thousands of voyages westward. Noting the earlier, less successful voyages, a good forecaster would have seen that the moment was ripe for an inflection point and could have advised the Portuguese that it would be unwise to turn down Columbus's request.

Ironically, forecasters can do worse than ordinary observers when it comes to anticipating inflection points. Ordinary folks are simply surprised when an inflection point arrives seemingly out of nowhere, but innovators and would-be forecasters who glimpse the flat-line beginnings of the S curve often miscalculate the speed at which the inflection point will arrive. As futurist Roy Amara pointed out to me three decades ago, there is a tendency to overestimate the short term and underestimate the long term. Our hopes cause us to conclude that the revolution will arrive overnight. Then, when cold reality fails to conform to our inflated expectations, our disappointment leads us to conclude that the hoped-for revolution will never arrive at all—right before it does.

One reason for the miscalculations is that the left-hand part of the S curve is much longer than most people imagine. Television took 20 years, plus time out for a war, to go from invention in the 1930s to takeoff in the early 1950s. Even in that hotbed of rapid change, Silicon Valley, most ideas take 20 years to become an overnight success. The Internet was almost 20 years old in 1988, the year that it began its dramatic run-up to the 1990s dot-com eruption. So having identified the origins and shape of the left-hand side of the S curve, you are always safer betting that events will unfold slowly than concluding that a sudden shift is in the wind. The best advice ever given to me was by a rancher who reminded me of an old bit of folk wisdom: "Son, never mistake a clear view for a short distance."

Once an inflection point arrives, people commonly underestimate the speed with which change will occur. The fact is, we are all by nature linear thinkers, and phenomena governed by the sudden, exponential growth of power laws catch us by surprise again and again. Even if we notice the beginning of a change, we instinctively draw a straight line diagonally through the S curve, and although we eventually arrive in the same spot, we miss both the lag at the start and the explosive growth in the middle. Timing, of course, is everything, and Silicon Valley is littered with the corpses of companies who mistook a clear view for a short distance and others who misjudged the magnitude of the S curve they happened upon.

Also expect the opportunities to be very different from those the majority predicts, for even the most expected futures tend to arrive in utterly unexpected ways. In the early 1980s, for example, PC makers predicted that every home would shortly have a PC on which people would do word processing and use spreadsheets or, later, read encyclopedias on CDs. But when home PC use did finally come about, it was driven by entertainment, not work, and when people finally consulted encyclopedias on-screen a decade after the PC makers said they would, the encyclopedias were online. The established companies selling their encyclopedias only on CD quickly went out of business.

Rule 3: Embrace the Things That Don't Fit

The novelist William Gibson once observed: "The future's already arrived. It's just not evenly distributed yet." The leading-edge line of an emerging S curve is like a string hanging down from the future, and the odd event you can't get out of your mind could be a weak signal of a distant industry-disrupting S curve just starting to gain momentum.

The entire portion of the S curve to the left of the inflection point is paved with indicators—subtle pointers that when aggregated become powerful hints of things to come. The best way for forecasters to spot an emerging S curve is to become attuned to things that don't fit, things people can't classify or will even reject. Because of our dislike of uncertainty and our preoccupation with the present, we tend to ignore indicators that don't fit into familiar boxes. But by definition anything that is truly new won't fit into a category that already exists.

A classic example is the first sales of characters and in-game objects from the online game EverQuest on eBay in the late 1990s. Though eBay banned these sales in 2001, they anticipated the recent explosive growth of commerce in Second Life, Linden Lab's virtual world in which members create 3-D avatars (digital alter egos). Through the avatars, members engage in social activities, including the creation and sale of in-world objects in a currency (Linden dollars) that can be exchanged for real dollars through various means. Today there are approximately 12 million subscribers participating in virtual world simulations like Second Life, and they're having an impact measurable in actual dollars. Real transactions connected with Second Life and other online simulations now are (conservatively) estimated at more than $1 billion annually. Where it ends is still uncertain, but it is unquestionably a very large S curve.

More often than not, indicators look like mere oddball curiosities or, worse, failures, and just as we dislike uncertainty, we shy away from failures and anomalies. But if you want to look for the thing that's going to come whistling in out of nowhere in the next years and change your business, look for interesting failures—smart ideas that seem to have gone nowhere.

Let's go back to Second Life. Its earliest graphical antecedent was Habitat, an online environment developed by Lucasfilm Games in 1985. Though nongraphical MUDs (multiple user dimensions) were a cultish niche success at the time, Habitat quickly disappeared, as did a string of other graphical MUDs developed in the 1980s and 1990s. Then the tide turned in the late 1990s, when multiplayer online games like EverQuest and Ultima started to take off. It was just a matter of time before the S curve that had begun with Habitat would spike for social environments as well as for games. Linden Lab's founders arrived on the scene with Second Life at the right time and with the right vision—that property ownership was the secret to success. (Sony missed this crucial point and insisted that everything in EverQuest, including user-created objects, was Sony's property, thus cutting EverQuest out of the wild sales-driven growth of virtual world simulations.) So although the explosive success of Second Life came as a considerable surprise to many people, from a forecasting perspective it arrived just about on time, almost 20 years after Habitat briefly appeared and expired.

As the Second Life example illustrates, indicators come in clusters. Here's another good example. Some readers will recall the flurry of news around the first two DARPA Grand Challenges, in which inventors and researchers were invited by the U.S. Department of Defense to design robots that could compete in a 100-mile-plus race across the Mojave Desert. The first Grand Challenge, which offered a $1 million prize, was held in March 2004. Most of the robots died in sight of the starting line, and only one robot got more than seven miles into the course. The Challenge's ambitious goal looked as remote as the summit of Everest. But just 19 months later, at the second Grand Challenge, five robots completed the course. Significantly, 19 months is approximately one doubling period under Moore's Law.

Around the same time I noticed a sudden new robot minicraze popping up that many people dismissed as just another passing fad. At the center of the craze was the Roomba, an inexpensive ($200 to $300) "smart" vacuum cleaner the size of a pizza pan. What was odd was that my friends with Roombas were as wildly enthusiastic about these machines as they had been about their original 128K Macs—and being engineers, they had never before shown any interest in owning, much less been excited by, a vacuum cleaner. Stranger yet, they gave their Roombas names, and when I checked with Roomba's maker, iRobot, I learned that in fact two-thirds of Roomba owners named their Roombas and one-third confessed to having taken their Roombas on vacation with them or over to friends houses to show them off.

Alone, this is just a curious story, but considered with the Grand Challenge success, it is another compelling indicator that a robotics inflection point lies in the not-too-distant future. What form this approaching robot revolution will take is still too uncertain to call, but I'll bet that it will be greeted with the same wild-eyed surprise and enthusiasm that greeted the rise of the PC in the early 1980s and the World Wide Web in the mid-1990s. Oh, and don't look for these robots to be the multitasking intelligent machines of science fiction. More likely, they'll be like the Roomba, more modest devices that do one or two tasks well or are simply cute and cuddly objects of affection. One indicator: Roomba owners today can even buy costumes for their robots!

Rule 4: Hold Strong Opinions Weakly

One of the biggest mistakes a forecaster—or a decision maker—can make is to overrely on one piece of seemingly strong information because it happens to reinforce the conclusion he or she has already reached. This lesson was tragically underscored when nine U.S. destroyers ran aground on the shores of central California on the fog-shrouded evening of September 8, 1923.

The lost ships were part of DesRon 11, a 14-ship squadron steaming from San Francisco to San Diego. Misled largely by overreliance on the commander's dead-reckoning navigation, the squadron undershot the turn into the Santa Barbara Channel and instead ended up on the rocks at Point Pedernales, several miles to the northwest.

The squadron had navigated by dead reckoning for most of the trip, but as the ships approached the channel, the squadron's commander obtained bearings from a radio direction station at Point Arguello. The bearing placed his ship, the *Delphy*, north of its dead reckoning position. Convinced that his dead reckoning was accurate, the commander reinterpreted the bearing data in a way that confirmed his erroneous position and ordered a sharp course change towards the rapidly approaching coast. Nine ships followed the disastrous course.

Meanwhile, the deck officers on the *Kennedy*, the 11th boat in the formation, had concluded from their dead reckoning that they in fact were farther north and closer to shore than the position given by the *Delphy*. The skipper was skeptical, but the doubt the deck officers raised was sufficient for him to hedge his bets; an hour before the fateful turn he ordered a course change that placed his ship several hundred yards to the west of the ships in front of them, allowing the *Kennedy* and the three trailing destroyers to avert disaster.

The essential difference between the two skippers' responses was that the *Delphy*'s skipper ignored evidence that invalidated his dead-reckoning information and narrowed his cone of uncertainty at the very moment when the data was screaming out to broaden it. In contrast, the *Kennedy*'s skipper listened to the multiple sources of conflicting weak information and concluded that his ship's position was much less certain than assumed. He hedged their bets and, therefore, saved the ship.

In forecasting, as in navigation, lots of interlocking weak information is vastly more trustworthy than a point or two of strong information. The problem is that traditional research habits are based on collecting strong information. And once researchers have gone through the long process of developing a beautiful hypothesis, they have a tendency to ignore any evidence that contradicts their conclusion. This inevitable resistance to contradictory information is responsible in no small part for the nonlinear process of paradigm shifts identified by Thomas Kuhn in his classic *The Structure of Scientific Revolutions*. Once a theory gains wide acceptance, there follows a long stable period in which the theory remains accepted wisdom. All the while, however, contradictory evidence is quietly building that eventually results in a sudden shift.

Good forecasting is the reverse: It is a process of strong opinions, weakly held. If you must forecast, then forecast often—and be the first one to prove yourself wrong. The way to do this is to form a forecast as quickly as possible and then set out to discredit it with new data. Let's say you are looking at the future cost of oil and its impact on the economy. Early on, you conclude that above a certain price point, say $80 a barrel, U.S. consumers will respond the way they did during the Carter administration, by putting on cardigans and conserving energy. Your next step is to try to find out why this might not happen. (So far it hasn't—perhaps because Americans are wealthier today, and, as evidenced by the past decade's strong SUV sales, they may not care deeply enough to change their habits on the basis of cost alone until the oil price is much higher.) By formulating a sequence of failed forecasts as rapidly as possible, you can steadily refine the cone of uncertainty to a point where you can comfortably base a strategic response on the forecast contained within its boundaries. Having

strong opinions gives you the capacity to reach conclusions quickly, but holding them weakly allows you to
discard them the moment you encounter conflicting
evidence.

Rule 5: Look Back Twice as Far as You Look Forward

Marshall McLuhan once observed that too often people
steer their way into the future while staring into the
rearview mirror because the past is so much more
comforting than the present. McLuhan was right, but
used properly, our historical rearview mirror is an
extraordinarily powerful forecasting tool. The texture of
past events can be used to connect the dots of present
indicators and thus reliably map the future's trajectory—
provided one looks back far enough.

Consider the uncertainty generated by the post-
bubble swirl of the Web, as incumbents like Google and
Yahoo, emergent players, and declining traditional TV
and print media players jockey for position. It all seems
to defy categorization, much less prediction, until one
looks back five decades to the emergence in the early
1950s of TV and the subsequent mass-media order it
helped catalyze. The present moment has eerie parallels
to that era, and inspection of those similarities quickly
brings today's landscape into sharp focus: We are in a
moment when the old mass-media order is being replaced
by a new personal-media order, and it's not just the
traditional media players that are struggling to adjust.
The cutting-edge players of the information revolution,
from Microsoft to Google, are pedaling every bit as hard.

The problem with history is that our love of certainty
and continuity often causes us to draw the wrong

conclusions. The recent past is rarely a reliable indicator of the future—if it were, one could successfully predict the next 12 months of the Dow or Nasdaq by laying a ruler along the past 12 months and extending the line forward. But the Dow doesn't behave that way, and neither does any other trend. You must look for the turns, not the straightaways, and thus you must peer far enough into the past to identify patterns. It's been written that "history doesn't repeat itself, but sometimes it rhymes." The effective forecaster looks to history to find the rhymes, not the identical events.

So when you look back for parallels, always look back at least twice as far as you are looking forward. Search for similar patterns, keeping in mind that history—especially recent history—rarely repeats itself directly. And don't be afraid to keep looking further back if the double interval is not enough to trigger your forecaster's informed intuition.

The hardest part of looking back is to know when history doesn't fit. The temptation is to use history (as the old analogy goes) the way a drunk uses a lamppost, for support rather than illumination. That's the single worst mistake a forecaster can make, and examples, unfortunately, abound. Jerry Levin, for instance, sold Time Warner to AOL in the mistaken belief that he could use mergers and acquisitions to shoulder his company into digital media the way he did so successfully with cable and movies. He ended up closing the deal just when AOL's decade-old model was being wiped out by new challengers with models allowing them to offer e-mail free of charge. Another case in point: A dark joke at the Pentagon is that the U.S. military is always fighting the last war, and indeed it is evident that in the case of the Iraq conflict, planners in certain areas simultaneously assumed that Iraq II would unfold like Iraq I and dismissed Vietnam as a source of insight because the U.S. had "lost that war."

Rule 6: Know When *Not* to Make a Forecast

It is a peculiar human quality that we are at once fearful of—and fascinated by—change. It is embedded in our social vocabulary, as we often greet a friend with the simple salutation, "What's new?" Yet it is a liability for forecasters to have too strong a proclivity to see change, for the simple fact is that even in periods of dramatic, rapid transformation, there are vastly more elements that do not change than new things that emerge.

Consider again that whirling vortex of the 1990s, the dot-com bubble. Plenty new was happening, but underlying the revolution were deep, unchanging consumer desires and ultimately, to the sorrow of many a start-up, unchanging laws of economics. By focusing on the novelties, many missed the fact that consumers were using their new broadband links to buy very traditional items like books and engage in old human activities like gossip, entertainment, and pornography. And though the future-lookers pronounced it to be a time when the old rules no longer applied, the old economic imperatives applied with a vengeance and the dot-com bubble burst just like every other bubble before it. Anyone who had taken the time to examine the history of economic bubbles would have seen it coming.

Against this backdrop, it is important to note that there are moments when forecasting is comparatively easy—and other moments when it is impossible. The cone of uncertainty is not static; it expands and contracts as the present rolls into the future and certain possibilities come to pass while others are closed off. There are thus moments of unprecedented uncertainty when the cone broadens to a point at which the wise forecaster will demur and refrain from making a forecast at all. But even in such a moment, one can take comfort in the knowledge that things will soon settle down, and with the careful exercise of intuition, it will once again be possible to make a good forecast.

Consider the events surrounding the fall of the Berlin Wall. In January 1989, the East German leader, Erich Honecker, declared that the wall would stand for "a hundred more years," and indeed Western governments built all their plans around this assumption. The signs of internal collapse are obvious in hindsight, but at the time, the world seemed locked in a bipolar superpower order that despite its nuclear fearfulness was remarkably stable. The cone of uncertainty, therefore, was relatively narrow, and within its boundaries there were a number of easily imaginable outcomes, including the horror of mutual destruction. Uncertainties popped up only where the two superpowers' spheres of influence touched and overlapped. But even here, there was a hierarchy of uncertainty: When change eventually came, it would likely unfold first in South Asia or restive Poland rather than in Berlin, safely encircled by its wall.

But the Berlin Wall came crashing down in the fall of 1989, and with it crumbled the certainty of a forecast rooted in the assumption of a world dominated by two superpowers. A comfortably narrow cone dilated to 180 degrees, and at that moment the wise forecaster would have refrained from jumping to conclusions and instead would have quietly looked for indicators of what would emerge from the geopolitical rubble—both overlooked indicators leading up to the wall's collapse and new ones emerging from its geopolitical detritus.

Indeed, the new order revealed itself within 12 months, and the indicator was Iraq's invasion of Kuwait on August 2, 1990. Before the collapse of the USSR, such an action would have triggered a Cuban Missile Crisis–like conflict between the two superpowers, but without a strong Soviet Union either to restrain Saddam or saber-rattle back, the outcome was very different. And with it, the new geopolitical order was obvious: The cone of uncertainty had narrowed to encompass a world where the myriad players once arrayed in the orderly force field of one superpower or another now were all going in their own directions. All the uncertainty shifted to center on whether the single surviving superpower could remain one at all. Iraq II of course has provided the answer to that question: A unipolar superpower order is not possible. As others have observed, we live in a world where the sole remaining superpower is too powerful to ignore but too weak to make a difference.

Bottom line? Be skeptical about apparent changes, and avoid making an immediate forecast—or at least don't take any one forecast too seriously. The incoming future will wash up plenty more indicators on your beach, sooner than you think.

Professional forecasters are developing ever more complex and subtle tools for peering ahead— futures markets, online expert aggregations, sophisticated computer-based simulations and even horizon-scanning software that crawls the Web looking for surprises. That is why it is essential for executives to become sophisticated and participative consumers of forecasts. That doesn't mean you must learn nonlinear algebra or become a forecasting expert in your own right. At the end of the day, forecasting is nothing more (nor less) than the systematic and disciplined application of common sense. It is the exercise of your own common sense that will allow you to assess the quality of the forecasts given to you—and to properly identify the opportunities and risks they present. But don't stop there. The best way to make sense of what lies ahead is to forecast for yourself.

Originally published in July 2007
Reprint R0707K

Strategy Under Uncertainty

HUGH COURTNEY, JANE KIRKLAND,
AND PATRICK VIGUERIE

Executive Summary

AT THE HEART of the traditional approach to
strategy lies the assumption that by applying a set
of powerful analytic tools, executives can predict
the future of any business accurately enough to
allow them to choose a clear strategic direction.
But what happens when the environment is so
uncertain that no amount of analysis will allow
us to predict the future? What makes for a good
strategy in highly uncertain business environments?

The authors, consultants at McKinsey &
Company, argue that uncertainty requires a new
way of thinking about strategy. All too often, they
say, executives take a binary view: either they
underestimate uncertainty to come up with the
forecasts required by their companies' planning
or capital-budgeting processes, or they overestimate

it, abandon all analysis, and go with their gut instinct.

The authors outline a new approach that begins by making a crucial distinction among four discrete levels of uncertainty that any company might face. They then explain how a set of generic strategies—shaping the market, adapting to it, or reserving the right to play at a later time—can be used in each of the four levels. And they illustrate how these strategies can be implemented through a combination of three basic types of actions: big bets, options, and no-regrets moves.

The framework can help managers determine which analytic tools can inform decision making under uncertainty—and which cannot. At a broader level, it offers executives a discipline for thinking rigorously and systematically about uncertainty and its implications for strategy.

W HAT MAKES FOR A GOOD STRATEGY in highly uncertain business environments? Some executives seek to shape the future with high-stakes bets. Eastman Kodak Company, for example, is spending $500 million per year to develop an array of digital photography products that it hopes will fundamentally change the way people create, store, and view pictures. Meanwhile, Hewlett-Packard Company is investing $50 million per year to pursue a rival vision centered around home-based photo printers. The business press loves to hype such industry-shaping strategies because of their potential to create enormous wealth, but the sober reality is that most companies lack the industry position, assets, or appetite for risk necessary to make such strategies work.

More risk-averse executives hedge their bets by making a number of smaller investments. In pursuit of growth opportunities in emerging markets, for example, many consumer-product companies are forging limited operational or distribution alliances. But it's often difficult to determine if such limited investments truly reserve the right to play in these countries or just reserve the right to lose.

Alternatively, some executives favor investments in flexibility that allow their companies to adapt quickly as markets evolve. But the costs of establishing such flexibility can be high. Moreover, taking a wait-and-see strategy—postponing large investments until the future becomes clear—can create a window of opportunity for competitors.

How should executives facing great uncertainty decide whether to bet big, hedge, or wait and see? Chances are, traditional strategic-planning processes won't help much. The standard practice is to lay out a vision of future events precise enough to be captured in a discounted-cash-flow analysis. Of course, managers can discuss alternative scenarios and test how sensitive their forecasts are to changes in key variables, but the goal of such analysis is often to find the most likely outcome and create a strategy based on it. That approach serves companies well in relatively stable business environments. But when there is greater uncertainty about the future, it is at best marginally helpful and at worst downright dangerous.

One danger is that this traditional approach leads executives to view uncertainty in a binary way—to assume that the world is either certain, and therefore open to precise predictions about the future, or uncertain, and therefore completely unpredictable. Planning or capital-budgeting processes that require point forecasts force managers to bury underlying uncertainties in their cash flows. Such systems clearly push managers to underestimate uncertainty in order to make a compelling case for their strategy.

Underestimating uncertainty can lead to strategies that neither defend against the threats nor take advantage of the opportunities that higher levels of uncertainty may provide. In one of the most colossal underestimations in business history, Kenneth H. Olsen, then president of Digital Equipment Corporation, announced in 1977 that "there is no reason for any individual to have a computer in their home." The explosion in the personal computer market was not inevitable in 1977, but it was certainly within the range of possibilities that industry experts were discussing at the time.

At the other extreme, assuming that the world is entirely unpredictable can lead managers to abandon the analytical rigor of their traditional planning processes altogether and base their strategic decisions primarily on gut instinct. This "just do it" approach to strategy can cause executives to place misinformed bets on emerging products or markets that result in record write-offs. Those who took the plunge and invested in home banking in the early 1980s immediately come to mind.

Risk-averse managers who think they are in very uncertain environments don't trust their gut instincts and suffer from decision paralysis. They avoid making critical strategic decisions about the products, markets, and technologies they should develop. They focus instead on reengineering, quality management, or internal cost-reduction programs. Although valuable, those programs are not substitutes for strategy.

Making systematically sound strategic decisions under uncertainty requires a different approach—one that avoids this dangerous binary view. It is rare that managers know absolutely nothing of strategic importance, even in the most uncertain environments. In fact, they usually can identify a range of potential outcomes or even a discrete set of scenarios. This simple insight is extremely powerful because determining which strategy is best, and what process should be used to develop it, depend vitally on the level of uncertainty a company faces.

What follows, then, is a framework for determining the level of uncertainty surrounding strategic decisions and for tailoring strategy to that uncertainty. No approach can make the challenges of uncertainty go away, but this one offers practical guidance that will lead to more informed and confident strategic decisions.

Four Levels of Uncertainty

Even the most uncertain business environments contain a lot of strategically relevant information. First, it is often possible to identify clear trends, such as market demographics, that can help define potential demand for future products or services. Second, there is usually a host of factors that are currently *unknown* but that are in fact *knowable*—that could be known if the right analysis were done. Performance attributes for current technologies, elasticities of demand for certain stable categories of products, and competitors' capacity-expansion plans are variables that are often unknown, but not entirely unknowable.

The uncertainty that remains after the best possible analysis has been done is what we call *residual uncertainty*—for example, the outcome of an ongoing regulatory debate or the performance attributes of a technology still in development. But often, quite a bit can be known about even those residual uncertainties. In practice, we have found that the residual uncertainty facing most strategic-decision makers falls into one of four broad levels.

LEVEL 1: A CLEAR-ENOUGH FUTURE

At level 1, managers can develop a single forecast of the future that is precise enough for strategy development. Although it will be inexact to the degree that all business environments are inherently uncertain, the forecast will be sufficiently narrow to point to a single strategic direction. In other words, at level 1, the residual uncertainty is irrelevant to making strategic decisions.

Consider a major airline trying to develop a strategic response to the entry of a low-cost, no-frills competitor into one of its hub airports. Should it respond with a low-cost service of its own? Should it cede the low-cost niche segments to the new entrant? Or should it compete aggressively on price and service in an attempt to drive the entrant out of the market?

To make that strategic decision, the airline's executives need market research on the size of different customer segments and the likely response of each segment to different combinations of pricing and service. They also need to know how much it costs the competitor to serve, and how much capacity the competitor has for, every route in question. Finally, the executives need to know the new entrant's competitive objectives to anticipate how it would respond to any strategic moves their airline might make. In today's U.S. airline industry, such information is either known already or is possible to know. It might not be easy to obtain—it might require new market research, for example—but it is inherently knowable. And once that information is known, residual uncertainty would be limited, and the incumbent airline would be able to build a confident business case around its strategy.

LEVEL 2: ALTERNATE FUTURES

At level 2, the future can be described as one of a few alternate outcomes, or *discrete scenarios*. Analysis cannot identify which outcome will occur, although it may help establish probabilities. Most important, some, if not all, elements of the strategy would change if the outcome were predictable.

Many businesses facing major regulatory or legislative change confront level 2 uncertainty. Consider U.S. long-distance telephone providers in late 1995, as they began developing strategies for entering local telephone markets. By late 1995, legislation that would fundamentally deregulate the industry was pending in Congress, and the broad form that new regulations would take was fairly clear to most industry observers. But whether or not the legislation was going to pass and how quickly it would be implemented in the event it did pass were uncertain. No amount of analysis would allow the long-distance carriers to predict those outcomes, and the correct course of action—for example, the timing of investments in network infrastructure—depended on which outcome occurred.

In another common level 2 situation, the value of a strategy depends mainly on competitors' strategies, and those cannot yet be observed or predicted. For example, in oligopoly markets, such as those for pulp and paper, chemicals, and basic raw materials, the primary uncertainty is often competitors' plans for expanding capacity: Will they build new plants or not? Economies of scale often dictate that any plant built would be quite large and would be likely to have a significant impact on industry prices and profitability. Therefore, any one company's decision to build a plant is often contingent on competitors' decisions. This is a classic level 2 situation: The possible outcomes are discrete and clear. It is difficult to predict which one will occur. And the best strategy depends on which one does occur.

LEVEL 3: A RANGE OF FUTURES

At level 3, a range of potential futures can be identified. That range is defined by a limited number of key variables, but the actual outcome may lie anywhere along a continuum bounded by that range. There are no natural discrete scenarios. As in level 2, some, and possibly all, elements of the strategy would change if the outcome were predictable.

Companies in emerging industries or entering new geographic markets often face level 3 uncertainty. Consider a European consumer-goods company deciding whether to introduce its products to the Indian market. The best possible market research might identify only a broad range of potential customer-penetration rates—say, from 10% to 30%—and there would be no obvious scenarios within that range. Such a broad range of estimates would be common when introducing completely new products and services to a market, and therefore determining the level of latent demand is very difficult. The company entering India would be likely to follow a very different and more aggressive entry strategy if it knew for certain that its customer penetration rates would be closer to 30% than to 10%.

Analogous problems exist for companies in fields driven by technological innovation, such as the semiconductor industry. When deciding whether to invest in a new technology, producers can often estimate only a broad range of potential cost and performance attributes for the technology, and the overall profitability of the investment depends on those attributes.

LEVEL 4: TRUE AMBIGUITY

At level 4, multiple dimensions of uncertainty interact to create an environment that is virtually impossible to predict. Unlike in level 3 situations, the range of potential outcomes cannot be identified, let alone scenarios within that range. It might not even be possible to identify, much less predict, all the relevant variables that will define the future.

Level 4 situations are quite rare, and they tend to migrate toward one of the other levels over time. Nevertheless, they do exist. Consider a telecommunications company deciding where and how to compete in the emerging consumer-multimedia market. It is confronting multiple uncertainties concerning technology, demand, and relationships between hardware and content providers, all of which may interact in ways so unpredictable that no plausible range of scenarios can be identified.

Companies considering making major entry investments in post-Communist Russia in 1992 faced level 4 uncertainty. They could not outline the potential laws or regulations that would govern property rights and transactions. That central uncertainty was compounded by additional uncertainty over the viability of supply chains and the demand for previously unavailable consumer goods and services. And shocks such as a political assassination or a currency default could have spun the whole system toward completely unforeseen outcomes.

Those examples illustrate how difficult strategic decisions can be at level 4, but they also underscore their transitory nature. Greater political and regulatory stability has turned decisions about whether to enter Russian markets into level 3 problems for the majority of industries today. Similarly, uncertainty about strategic decisions in the consumer multimedia market will migrate to level 3 or to level 2 as the industry begins to take shape over the next several years.

Tailoring Strategic Analysis to the Four Levels of Uncertainty

Our experience suggests that at least half of all strategy problems fall into levels 2 or 3, while most of the rest are level 1 problems. But executives who think about uncertainty in a binary way tend to treat all strategy problems as if they fell into either level 1 or level 4. And when those executives base their strategies on rigorous analysis, they are most likely to apply the same set of analytic tools regardless of the level of residual uncertainty they face.

How to Use the Four Levels of Uncertainty

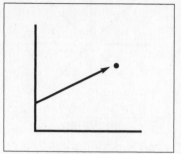

A Clear-Enough Future

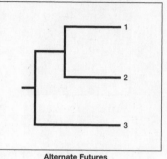

Alternate Futures

	A Clear-Enough Future	**Alternate Futures**
What Can Be Known?	• A single forecast precise enough for determining strategy	• A few discrete outcomes that define the future
Analytic Tools	• "Traditional" strategy tool kit	• Decision analysis • Option valuation models • Game theory
Examples	• Strategy against low-cost airline entrant	• Long-distance telephone carriers' strategy to enter deregulated local-service market • Capacity strategies for chemical plants

For example, they might attempt to use standard, quantitative market-research techniques to forecast demand for data traffic over wireless communications networks as far out as ten years from now.

But, in fact, a different kind of analysis should be done to identify and evaluate strategy options at each level of uncertainty. All strategy making begins with some form of situation analysis—that is, a picture of what the world will look like today and what is likely to happen in the future. Identifying the levels of uncertainty thus helps

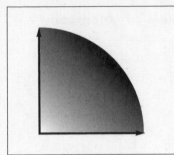

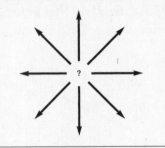

	A Range of Future	**True Ambiguity**

	A Range of Futures	**True Ambiguity**
What Can Be Known?	• A range of possible outcomes, but no natural scenarios	• No basis to forecast the future
Analytic Tools	• Latent-demand research • Technology forecasting • Scenario planning	• Analogies and pattern recognition • Nonlinear dynamic models
Examples	• Entering emerging markets, such as India • Developing or acquiring emerging technologies in consumer electronics	• Entering the market for consumer multimedia applications • Entering the Russian market in 1992

define the best such an analysis can do to describe each possible future an industry faces.

To help generate level 1's usefully precise prediction of the future, managers can use the standard strategy tool kit—market research, analyses of competitors' costs and capacity, value chain analysis, Michael Porter's five-forces framework, and so on. A discounted-cash-flow model that incorporates those predictions can then be used to determine the value of various alternative strategies. It's not surprising that most managers feel extremely comfortable in level 1 situations—these are the tools and frameworks taught in every leading business program in the United States.

Level 2 situations are a bit more complex. First, managers must develop a set of discrete scenarios based on their understanding of how the key residual uncertainties might play out—for example, whether deregulation occurs or not, a competitor builds a new plant or not. Each scenario may require a different valuation model— general industry structure and conduct will often be fundamentally different depending on which scenario occurs, so alternative valuations can't be handled by performing sensitivity analyses around a single baseline model. Getting information that helps establish the relative probabilities of the alternative outcomes should be a high priority.

After establishing an appropriate valuation model for each possible outcome and determining how probable each is likely to be, a classic decision-analysis framework can be used to evaluate the risks and returns inherent in alternative strategies. This process will identify the likely winners and losers in alternative scenarios, and perhaps more important, it will help quantify what's at stake for companies that follow status quo strategies. Such an analysis is often the key to making the case for strategic change.

In level 2 situations, it is important not only to identify the different possible future outcomes but also to think through the likely paths the industry might take to reach those alternative futures. Will change occur in major steps at some particular point in time, following, for example, a regulatory ruling or a competitor's decision to enter the market? Or will change occur in a more evolutionary fashion, as often happens after a resolution of competing technology standards? This is vital information because it determines which market signals or trigger variables should be monitored closely. As events unfold and the relative probabilities of alternative scenarios change, it is likely that one's strategy will also need to be adapted to these changes.

At one level, the analysis in level 3 is very similar to that in level 2. A set of scenarios needs to be identified that describes alternative future outcomes, and analysis should focus on the trigger events signaling that the market is moving toward one or another scenario. Developing a meaningful set of scenarios, however, is less straightforward in level 3. Scenarios that describe the extreme points in the range of possible outcomes are often relatively easy to develop, but these rarely provide much concrete guidance for current strategic decisions. Since there are no other natural discrete scenarios in level 3, deciding which possible outcomes should be fully developed into alternative scenarios is a real art. But there are a few general rules. First, develop only a limited number of alternative scenarios—the complexity of juggling more than four or five tends to hinder decision making. Second, avoid developing redundant scenarios that have no unique implications for strategic decision making; make sure each scenario offers a distinct picture of the industry's structure, conduct, and performance. Third, develop a set of scenarios that collectively account for the *probable* range of future outcomes and not necessarily the entire *possible* range.

Because it is impossible in level 3 to define a complete list of scenarios and related probabilities, it is impossible to calculate the expected value of different strategies. However, establishing the range of scenarios should allow managers to determine how robust their strategy is, identify likely winners and losers, and determine roughly the risk of following status quo strategies.

Situation analysis at level 4 is even more qualitative. Still, it is critical to avoid the urge to throw one's hands up and act purely on gut instinct. Instead, managers need to catalog systematically what they know and what is possible to know. Even if it is impossible to develop a meaningful set of probable, or even possible, outcomes in level 4 situations, managers can gain valuable strategic perspective. Usually, they can identify at least a subset of the variables that will determine how the market will evolve over time—for example, customer penetration rates or technology performance attributes. And they can identify favorable and unfavorable indicators of these variables that will let them track the market's evolution over time and adapt their strategy as new information becomes available.

Managers can also identify patterns indicating possible ways the market may evolve by studying how analogous markets developed in other level 4 situations, determining the key attributes of the winners and losers in those situations and identifying the strategies they employed. Finally, although it will be impossible to quantify the risks and returns of different strategies, managers should be able to identify what information they would have to believe about the future to justify the investments they are considering. Early market indicators and analogies from similar markets will help sort out whether such beliefs are realistic or not.

Uncertainty demands a more flexible approach to situation analysis. The old one-size-fits-all approach is simply inadequate. Over time, companies in most industries will face strategy problems that have varying levels of residual uncertainty, and it is vitally important that the strategic analysis be tailored to the level of uncertainty.

Postures and Moves

Before we can talk about the dynamics of formulating strategy at each level of uncertainty, we need to introduce a basic vocabulary for talking about strategy. First, there are three *strategic postures* a company can choose to take vis-à-vis uncertainty: shaping, adapting, or reserving the right to play. Second, there are three types of moves in *the portfolio of actions* that can be used to implement that strategy: big bets, options, and no-regrets moves.

STRATEGIC POSTURE

Any good strategy requires a choice about strategic posture. Fundamentally, *posture* defines the intent of a strategy relative to the current and future state of an industry. *Shapers* aim to drive their industries toward a new structure of their own devising. Their strategies are about creating new opportunities in a market—either by shaking up relatively stable level 1 industries or by trying to control the direction of the market in industries with higher levels of uncertainty. Kodak, for example, through

---

The Three Strategic Postures

Shape the future

Play a leadership role in establishing how the industry operates, for example:
• setting standards
• creating demand

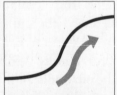

Adapt to the future

Win through speed, agility, and flexibiltiy in recognizing and capturing opportunities in existing markets

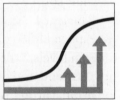

Reserve the right to play

Invest sufficiently to stay in the game but avoid premature commitments

its investment in digital photography, is pursuing a
shaping strategy in an effort to maintain its leadership
position, as a new technology supersedes the one currently generating most of its earnings. Although its
product technology is new, Kodak's strategy is still based
on a traditional model in which the company provides
digital cameras and film while photo-processing stores
provide many of the photo-printing and storage functions for the consumer. Hewlett-Packard also seeks to
be a shaper in this market, but it is pursuing a radically
different model in which high-quality, low-cost photo
printers shift photo processing from stores to the home.

In contrast, *adapters* take the current industry structure and its future evolution as givens, and they react to
the opportunities the market offers. In environments
with little uncertainty, adapters choose a strategic
positioning—that is, where and how to compete—in
the current industry. At higher levels of uncertainty,
their strategies are predicated on the ability to recognize
and respond quickly to market developments. In the
highly volatile telecommunications-service industry,
for example, service resellers are adapters. They buy
and resell the latest products and services offered by
the major telecom providers, relying on pricing and
effective execution rather than on product innovation
as their source of competitive advantage.

The third strategic posture, *reserving the right to play*,
is a special form of adapting. This posture is relevant
only in levels 2 through 4; it involves making incremental
investments today that put a company in a privileged
position, through either superior information, cost structures, or relationships between customers and suppliers.
That allows the company to wait until the environment
becomes less uncertain before formulating a strategy.

Many pharmaceutical companies are reserving the right to play in the market for gene therapy applications by acquiring or allying with small biotech firms that have relevant expertise. Providing privileged access to the latest industry developments, these are low-cost investments compared with building a proprietary, internal gene-therapy R&D program.

A PORTFOLIO OF ACTIONS

A posture is not a complete strategy. It clarifies strategic intent but not the actions required to fulfill that intent. Three types of moves are especially relevant to implementing strategy under conditions of uncertainty: big bets, options, and no-regrets moves.

Big bets are large commitments, such as major capital investments or acquisitions, that will result in large payoffs in some scenarios and large losses in others. Not surprisingly, shaping strategies usually involve big bets, whereas adapting and reserving the right to play do not.

What's in a Portfolio of Actions?

These building blocks are distinguished by three payoff profiles—that is, the amount of investment required up front and the conditions under which the investment will yield a positive return.

Scenario	Value
1.	+
2.	+
3.	+
4.	+

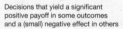

No-regrets moves

Strategic decisions that have positive payoffs in any scenario

Options

Decisions that yield a significant positive payoff in some outcomes and a (small) negative effect in others

Big bets

Focused strategies with positive payoffs in one or more scenarios but a negative effect in others

Options are designed to secure the big payoffs of the best-case scenarios while minimizing losses in the worst-case scenarios. This asymmetric payoff structure makes them resemble financial options. Most options involve making modest initial investments that will allow companies to ramp up or scale back the investment later as the market evolves. Classic examples include conducting pilot trials before the full-scale introduction of a new product, entering into limited joint ventures for distribution to minimize the risk of breaking into new markets, and licensing an alternative technology in case it proves to be superior to a current technology. Those reserving the right to play rely heavily on options, but shapers use them as well, either to shape an emerging but uncertain market as an early mover or to hedge their big bets.

Finally, *no-regrets moves* are just that—moves that will pay off no matter what happens. Managers often focus on obvious no-regrets moves like initiatives aimed at reducing costs, gathering competitive intelligence, or building skills. However, even in highly uncertain environments, strategic decisions like investing in capacity and entering certain markets can be no-regrets moves. Whether or not they put a name to them, most managers understand intuitively that no-regrets moves are an essential element of any strategy.

The choice of a strategic posture and an accompanying portfolio of actions sounds straightforward. But in practice, these decisions are highly dependent on the level of uncertainty facing a given business. Thus the four-level framework can help clarify the practical implications implicit in any choice of strategic posture and actions. The discussion that follows will demonstrate the different strategic challenges that each level of uncertainty poses and how the portfolio of actions may be applied.

STRATEGY IN LEVEL 1'S
CLEAR-ENOUGH FUTURE

In predictable business environments, most companies are adapters. Analysis is designed to predict an industry's future landscape, and strategy involves making positioning choices about where and how to compete. When the underlying analysis is sound, such strategies are by definition made up of a series of no-regrets moves.

Adapter strategies in level 1 situations are not necessarily incremental or boring. For example, Southwest Airlines Company's no-frills, point-to-point service is a highly innovative, value-creating adapter strategy, as was Gateway 2000's low-cost assembly and direct-mail distribution strategy when it entered the personal computer market in the late 1980s. In both cases, managers were able to identify unexploited opportunities in relatively low-uncertainty environments within the existing market structure. The best level 1 adapters create value through innovations in their products or services or through improvements in their business systems without otherwise fundamentally changing the industry.

It is also possible to be a shaper in level 1 situations, but that is risky and rare, since level 1 shapers increase the amount of residual uncertainty in an otherwise predictable market—for themselves and their competitors—in an attempt to fundamentally alter long-standing industry structures and conduct. Consider Federal Express Corporation's overnight-delivery strategy. When it entered the mail-and-package delivery industry, a stable level 1 situation, FedEx's strategy in effect created level 3 uncertainty for itself. That is, even though CEO Frederick W. Smith commissioned detailed consulting reports that confirmed the feasibility of his business concept, only a broad range of potential demand for overnight services could be identified at the time. For the industry incumbents like United Parcel Service, FedEx created level 2 uncertainty. FedEx's move raised two questions for UPS: Will the overnight-delivery strategy succeed or not? and Will UPS have to offer a similar service to remain a viable competitor in the market?

Over time, the industry returned to level 1 stability, but with a fundamentally new structure. FedEx's bet paid off, forcing the rest of the industry to adapt to the new demand for overnight services.

What portfolio of actions did it take to realize that strategy? Like most shaper strategies, even in level 1 situations, this one required some big bets. That said, it often makes sense to build options into a shaper strategy to hedge against bad bets. Smith might have hedged his bets by leasing existing cargo airplanes instead of purchasing and retrofitting his original fleet of Falcon "minifreighters," or he could have outsourced ground pickup and delivery services. Such moves would have limited the amount of capital he would have needed to sink into his new strategy and facilitated a graceful exit had his concept failed. However, that kind of insurance doesn't always come cheap. In FedEx's case, had Smith leased standard-size cargo planes, he would have come under the restrictive regulations of the Civil Aeronautics Board. And outsourcing local pickups and deliveries would have diluted FedEx's unique door-to-door value to customers. Thus Smith stuck mainly to big bets in implementing his strategy, which drove him to the brink of bankruptcy in his first two years of operation but ultimately reshaped an entire industry.

STRATEGY IN LEVEL 2'S
ALTERNATE FUTURES

If shapers in level 1 try to raise uncertainty, in levels 2 through 4 they try to lower uncertainty and create order out of chaos. In level 2, a shaping strategy is designed to increase the probability that a favored industry scenario will occur. A shaper in a capital-intensive industry like pulp and paper, for example, wants to prevent competitors from creating excess capacity that would destroy the industry's profitability. Consequently, shapers in such cases might commit their companies to building new capacity far in advance of an upturn in demand to preempt the competition, or they might consolidate the industry through mergers and acquisitions.

Consider the Microsoft Network (MSN). A few years ago, one could identify a discrete set of possible ways in which transactions would be conducted between networked computers. Either proprietary networks such as MSN would become the standard, or open networks like the Internet would prevail. Uncertainty in this situation was thus at level 2, even though other related strategy issues—such as determining the level of consumer demand for networked applications—were level 3 problems.

Microsoft could reasonably expect to shape the way markets for electronic commerce evolved if it created the proprietary MSN network. It would, in effect, be building a commerce hub that would link both suppliers and consumers through the MSN gateway. The strategy was a big bet: the development costs were significant and, more important, involved an enormously high level of industry exposure and attention. In effect, for Microsoft, it constituted a big credibility bet. Microsoft's activities in other areas—such as including one-button access to MSN from Windows95—were designed to increase the probability that this shaping bet would pay off.

But even the best shapers must be prepared to adapt. In the battle between proprietary and open networks, certain trigger variables—growth in the number of Internet and MSN subscribers, for example, or the activity profiles of early MSN subscribers—could provide valuable insight into how the market was evolving. When it became clear that open networks would prevail, Microsoft refocused the MSN concept around the Internet. Microsoft's shift illustrates that choices of strategic posture are not carved in stone, and it underscores the value of maintaining strategic flexibility under uncertainty. Shaping strategies can fail, so the best companies supplement their shaping bets with options that allow them to change course quickly if necessary. Microsoft was able to do just that because it remained flexible by being willing to cut its losses, by building a cadre of engineers who had a wide range of general-programming and product-development skills, and by closely monitoring key trigger variables. In uncertain environments, it is a mistake to let strategies run on autopilot, remaining content to update them only through standard year-end strategy reviews.

Because trigger variables are often relatively simple to monitor in level 2, it can be easy to adapt or reserve the right to play. For instance, companies that generate electricity—and others whose business depends on energy-intensive production processes—often face level 2 uncertainty in determining the relative cost of different fuel alternatives. Discrete scenarios can often be identified—for example, either natural gas or oil will be the low-cost fuel. Many companies thus choose an adapter strategy when building new plants: they construct flexible manufacturing processes that can switch easily between different fuels.

Chemical companies often choose to reserve the right to play when facing level 2 uncertainty in predicting the performance of a new technology. If the technology performs well, companies will have to employ it to remain competitive in the market. But if it does not fulfill its promise, incumbents can compete effectively with existing technologies. Most companies are reluctant to bet several hundred million dollars on building new capacity and retrofitting old plants around a new technology until it is proven. But if they don't make at least incremental investments in the short run, they risk falling too far behind competitors should the technology succeed. Thus many will purchase options to license the new technology within a specified time frame or begin retrofitting a proportion of existing capacity around the new technology. In either case, small, up-front commitments give the companies privileged positions, but not obligations, to ramp up or discontinue development of the new technology as its performance attributes become clearer over time.

STRATEGY IN LEVEL 3'S RANGE OF FUTURES

Shaping takes a different form in level 3. If at level 2, shapers are trying to make a discrete outcome occur, at level 3, they are trying to move the market in a general direction because they can identify only a range of possible outcomes. Consider the battle over standards for electronic cash transactions, currently a level 3 problem since one can define a range of potential products and services that fall between purely paper-based and purely electronic cash transactions, but it is unclear today whether there are any natural discrete scenarios within that range. Mondex International, a consortium of financial services providers and technology companies, is attempting to shape the future by establishing what it hopes will become universal electronic-cash standards. Its shaping posture is backed by big-bet investments in product development, infrastructure, and pilot experiments to speed customer acceptance.

In contrast, regional banks are mainly choosing adapter strategies. An adapter posture at uncertainty levels 3 or 4 is often achieved primarily through investments in organizational capabilities designed to keep options open. Because they must make and implement strategy choices in real time, adapters need quick access to the best market information and the most flexible organizational structures. Many regional banks, for example, have put in place steering committees focused on electronic payments, R&D projects, and competitive-intelligence systems so that they can constantly monitor developments in electronic payment technology and markets. In addition, many regional banks are making small investments in industry consortia as another way to monitor events. This adapter approach makes sense for most regional banks—they don't have the deep pockets and skills necessary to set standards for the electronic payment market, yet it is essential that they be able to offer the latest electronic services to their customers as such services become available.

Reserving the right to play is a common posture in level 3. Consider a telecommunications company trying to decide whether to make a $1 billion investment in broadband cable networks in the early 1990s. The decision hinged on level 3 uncertainties such as demand for interactive TV service. No amount of solid market research could precisely forecast consumer demand for services that didn't even exist yet. However, making incremental investments in broadband-network trials could provide useful information, and it would put the company in a privileged position to expand the business in the future should that prove attractive. By restructuring the broadband-investment decision from a big bet to a series of options, the company reserved the right to play in a potentially lucrative market without having to bet the farm or risk being preempted by a competitor.

How a Regional Bank Confronts the Uncertainties in Electronic Commerce

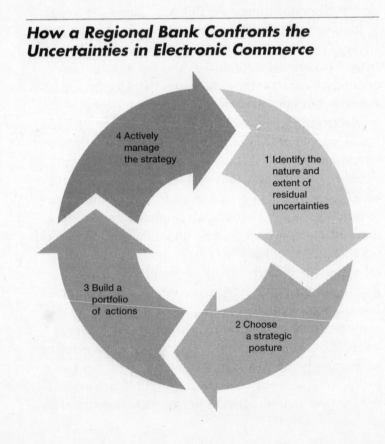

4 Actively manage the strategy

1 Identify the nature and extent of residual uncertainties

3 Build a portfolio of actions

2 Choose a strategic posture

1. Identify the nature and extent of residual uncertainties

Key areas of uncertainty include:

- How much electronic commerce will occur on the Internet
- How quickly consumers will switch from paper-based to electronic payments
- Which specific instruments will become the primary payment vehicles (smart cards? E-cash?)
- What structure will emerge for the electronic commerce industry
- How vertically integrated most players will be
- What roles banks and nonbanks will play

The bank is facing level 3 uncertainty in some areas and level 4 in others

2. Choose a strategic posture

Objectives:

- Defend current customer franchise from attack by new technology-based competitors
- Capture new business opportunities in fast growing markets

Overall posture: reserve the right to play

3. Build a portfolio of actions

Near-term opportunities to offer more innovative products in specific areas where the bank is strong (for example, procurement cards, industry-specific payment products) represent no-regrets moves.

Offering leading-edge payment products to high-value customer segments that are most vulnerable to attackers is another no-regrets move.

Forming a small new-business unit is a growth option to:

- Conduct R&D for new payment ideas
- Monitor industry developments in the broad area of retail electronic payments

4. Actively manage the strategy

Monitor key trigger events such as adoption rates for emerging products and the behavior of nontraditional competitors such as telephone companies.

Establish a short-cycle review of the portfolio of options.

Participate in a number of industry consortia to reduce uncertainty.

STRATEGY IN LEVEL 4'S TRUE AMBIGUITY

Paradoxically, even though level 4 situations contain the greatest uncertainty, they may offer higher returns and involve lower risks for companies seeking to shape the market than situations in either level 2 or 3. Recall that level 4 situations are transitional by nature, often occurring after a major technological, macroeconomic, or legislative shock. Since no player necessarily knows the best strategy in these environments, the shaper's role is to provide a vision of an industry structure and standards that will coordinate the strategies of other players and drive the market toward a more stable and favorable outcome.

Mahathir bin Mohamad, Malaysia's prime minister, is trying to shape the future of the multimedia industry in the Asian Pacific Rim. This is truly a level 4 strategy problem at this point. Potential products are undefined, as are the players, the level of customer demand, and the technology standards, among other factors. The government is trying to create order out of this chaos by investing at least $15 billion to create a so-called Multimedia Super Corridor (MSC) in Malaysia. The MSC is a 750-square-kilometer zone south of Kuala Lumpur that will include state-of-the-art "smart" buildings for software companies, regional headquarters for multinational corporations, a "Multimedia University," a paperless government center called Putrajaya, and a new city called Cyberjaya. By leveraging incentives like a ten-year exemption from the tax on profits, the MSC has received commitments from more than 40 Malaysian and foreign companies so far, including such powerhouses as Intel, Microsoft, Nippon Telegraph and Telephone, Oracle, and Sun Microsystems. Mahathir's shaping strategy is predicated on the notion that the

MSC will create a web of relationships between content and hardware providers that will result in clear industry standards and a set of complementary multimedia products and services. Intel's Malaysia managing director, David B. Marsing, recognized Mahathir's shaping aspirations when he noted, "If you're an evolutionist, it's strange. They're [the Malaysian government] trying to intervene instead of letting it evolve."

Shapers need not make enormous bets as the Malaysian government is doing to be successful in level 3 or 4 situations, however. All that is required is the credibility to coordinate the strategies of different players around the preferred outcome. Netscape Communications Corporation, for example, didn't rely on deep pockets to shape Internet browser standards. Instead, it leveraged the credibility of its leadership team in the industry so that other industry players thought, "If these guys think this is the way to go, they must be right."

Reserving the right to play is common, but potentially dangerous, in level 4 situations. Oil companies believed they were reserving the right to compete in China by buying options to establish various beachheads there some 20 years ago. However, in such level 4 situations, it is extremely difficult to determine whether incremental investments are truly reserving the right to play or simply the right to lose. A few general rules apply. First, look for a high degree of leverage. If the choice of beachhead in China comes down to maintaining a small, but expensive, local operation or developing a limited joint venture with a local distributor, all else being equal, go for the low-cost option. Higher-cost options must be justified with explicit arguments for why they would put the company in a better position to ramp up over time. Second,

don't get locked into one position through neglect.
Options should be rigorously reevaluated whenever
important uncertainties are clarified—at least every six
months. Remember, level 4 situations are transitional,
and most will quickly move toward levels 3 and 2.

The difficulty of managing options in level 4 situations often drives players toward adapter postures. As in
level 3, an adapter posture in level 4 is frequently implemented by making investments in organizational capabilities. Most potential players in the multimedia
industry are adopting that posture today but will soon be
making bigger bets as the industry moves into level 3 and
2 uncertainty over time.

A New Approach to Uncertainty

At the heart of the traditional approach to strategy
lies the assumption that by applying a set of powerful
analytic tools, executives can predict the future of any
business accurately enough to allow them to choose a
clear strategic direction. In relatively stable businesses,
that approach continues to work well. But it tends to
break down when the environment is so uncertain that
no amount of good analysis will allow them to predict
the future.

Levels of uncertainty regularly confronting managers
today are so high that they need a new way to think
about strategy. The approach we've outlined will help
executives avoid dangerous binary views of uncertainty.
It offers a discipline for thinking rigorously and systematically about uncertainty. On one plane, it is a guide to
judging which analytic tools can help in making decisions at various levels of uncertainty and which cannot.

On a broader plane, our framework is a way to tackle the most challenging decisions that executives have to make, offering a more complete and sophisticated understanding of the uncertainty they face and its implications for strategy.

Originally published in November 1997
Reprint 97603

A Leader's Framework for Decision Making

DAVID J. SNOWDEN AND MARY E. BOONE

Executive Summary

MANY EXECUTIVES ARE SURPRISED when previously successful leardership approaches fail in new situations, but different contexts call for different kinds of responses. Before addressing a situation, leaders need to recognize which context governs it—and tailor their actions accordingly.

Snowden and Boone have formed a new perspective on leadership and decision making that's based on complexity science. The result is the Cynefin framework, which helps executives sort issues into five contexts:

Simple contexts are characterized by stability and cause-and-effect relationships that are clear to everyone. Often, the right answer is self-evident.

In this realm of "known knowns," leaders must first assess the facts of a situation—that is, "sense" it— then categorize and respond to it.

Complicated contexts may contain multiple right answers, and though there is a clear relationship between cause and effect, not everyone can see it. This is the realm of "known unknowns." Here, leaders must sense, analyze, and respond.

In a *Complex* context, right answers can't be ferreted out at all; rather, instructive patterns emerge if the leader conducts experiments that can safely fail. This is the realm of "unknown unknowns," where much of contemporary business operates. Leaders in this context need to probe first, then sense, and then respond.

In a *chaotic* context, searching for right answers is pointless. The relationships between cause and effect are impossible to determine because they shift constantly and no manageable patterns exist. This is the realm of unknowables (the events of September 11, 2001, fall into this category). In this domain, a leader must first act to establish order, sense where stability is present, and then work to transform the situation from chaos to complexity.

The fifth context, *disorder*, applies when it is unclear which of the other four contexts is predominant. The way out is to break the situation into its constituent parts and assign each to one of the other four realms. Leaders can then make decisions and intervene in contextually appropriate ways.

I N JANUARY 1993, a gunman murdered seven people in a fast-food restaurant in Palatine, a suburb of Chicago. In his dual roles as an administrative executive and spokesperson for the police department, Deputy Chief Walter Gasior suddenly had to cope with several different situations at once. He had to deal with the grieving families and a frightened community, help direct the operations of an extremely busy police department, and take questions from the media, which inundated the town with reporters and film crews. "There would literally be four people coming at me with logistics and media issues all at once," he recalls. "And in the midst of all this, we still had a department that had to keep running on a routine basis."

Though Gasior was ultimately successful in juggling multiple demands, not all leaders achieve the desired results when they face situations that require a variety of decisions and responses. All too often, managers rely on common leadership approaches that work well in one set of circumstances but fall short in others. Why do these approaches fail even when logic indicates they should prevail? The answer lies in a fundamental assumption of organizational theory and practice: that a certain level of predictability and order exists in the world. This assumption, grounded in the Newtonian science that underlies scientific management, encourages simplifications that are useful in ordered circumstances. Circumstances change, however, and as they become more complex, the simplifications can fail. Good leadership is not a one-size-fits-all proposition.

We believe the time has come to broaden the traditional approach to leadership and decision making and form a new perspective based on complexity science.

(For more on this, see the insert "Understanding Complexity.") Over the past ten years, we have applied the principles of that science to governments and a broad range of industries. Working with other contributors, we developed the Cynefin framework, which allows executives to see things from new viewpoints, assimilate complex concepts, and address real-world problems and opportunities. (*Cynefin*, pronounced ku-*nev*-in, is a Welsh word that signifies the multiple factors in our environment and our experience that influence us in ways we can never understand.) Using this approach, leaders learn to define the framework with examples from their own organization's history and scenarios of its possible future. This enhances communication and helps executives rapidly understand the context in which they are operating.

The U.S. Defense Advanced Research Projects Agency has applied the framework to counterterrorism, and it is currently a key component of Singapore's Risk Assessment and Horizon Scanning program. Over time, the framework has evolved through hundreds of applications, from helping a pharmaceutical company develop a new product strategy to assisting a Canadian provincial government in its efforts to engage employees in policy making.

The framework sorts the issues facing leaders into five contexts defined by the nature of the relationship between cause and effect. Four of these—simple, complicated, complex, and chaotic—require leaders to diagnose situations and to act in contextually appropriate ways. The fifth—disorder—applies when it is unclear which of the other four contexts is predominant.

Using the Cynefin framework can help executives sense which context they are in so that they can not only make better decisions but also avoid the problems that arise when their preferred management style causes them to make mistakes. In this article, we focus on the first four contexts, offering examples and suggestions about how to lead and make appropriate decisions in

---

The Cynefin Framework

The Cynefin framework helps leaders determine the prevailing operative context so that they can make appropriate choices. Each domain requires different actions. *Simple* and *complicated* contexts assume an ordered universe, where cause-and-effect relationships are perceptible, and right answers can be determined based on the facts. *Complex* and *chaotic* contexts are unordered—there is no immediately apparent relationship between cause and effect, and the way forward is determined based on emerging patterns. The ordered world is the world of fact-based management; the unordered world represents pattern-based management.

The very nature of the fifth context—*disorder*—makes it particularly difficult to recognize when one is in it. Here, multiple perspectives jostle for prominence, factional leaders argue with one another, and cacophony rules. The way out of this realm is to break down the situation into constituent parts and assign each to one of the other four realms. Leaders can then make decisions and intervene in contextually appropriate ways.

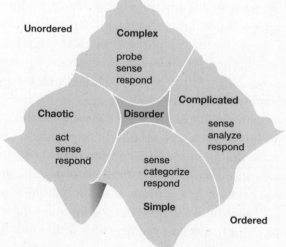

each of them. Since the complex domain is much more prevalent in the business world than most leaders realize—and requires different, often counterintuitive, responses—we concentrate particularly on that context. Leaders who understand that the world is often irrational and unpredictable will find the Cynefin framework particularly useful.

Simple Contexts: The Domain of Best Practice

Simple contexts are characterized by stability and clear cause-and-effect relationships that are easily discernible by everyone. Often, the right answer is self-evident and undisputed. In this realm of "known knowns," decisions are unquestioned because all parties share an understanding. Areas that are little subject to change, such as problems with order processing and fulfillment, usually belong here.

Simple contexts, properly assessed, require straightforward management and monitoring. Here, leaders *sense*, *categorize*, and *respond*. That is, they assess the facts of the situation, categorize them, and then base their response on established practice. Heavily process-oriented situations, such as loan payment processing, are often simple contexts. If something goes awry, an employee can usually identify the problem (when, say, a borrower pays less than is required), categorize it (review the loan documents to see how partial payments must be processed), and respond appropriately (either not accept the payment or apply the funds according to the terms of the note). Since both managers and employees have access to the information necessary for dealing with the situation in this domain, a command-and-control style for setting parameters works best. Directives are straightforward, decisions can be easily delegated, and functions are automated. Adhering to best practices or process reengineering makes sense. Exhaustive communication among managers and employees is not usually required because disagreement about what needs to be done is rare.

Nevertheless, problems can arise in simple contexts. First, issues may be incorrectly classified within this domain because they have been oversimplified. Leaders who constantly ask for condensed information, regardless of the complexity of the situation, particularly run this risk.

Second, leaders are susceptible to *entrained thinking*, a conditioned response that occurs when people are blinded to new ways of thinking by the perspectives they acquired through past experience, training, and success.

Third, when things appear to be going smoothly, leaders often become complacent. If the context changes at that point, a leader is likely to miss what is happening and react too late. In the exhibit "The Cynefin Framework," the simple domain lies adjacent to the chaotic— and for good reason. The most frequent collapses into chaos occur because success has bred complacency. This shift can bring about catastrophic failure—think of the many previously dominant technologies that were suddenly disrupted by more dynamic alternatives.

Leaders need to avoid micromanaging and stay connected to what is happening in order to spot a change in context. By and large, line workers in a simple situation are more than capable of independently handling any issues that may arise. Indeed, those with years of experience also have deep insight into how the work should be done. Leaders should create a communication channel—an anonymous one, if necessary—that allows dissenters to provide early warnings about complacency.

Finally, it's important to remember that best practice is, by definition, past practice. Using best practices is common, and often appropriate, in simple contexts. Difficulties arise, however, if staff members are discouraged from bucking the process even when it's not working anymore. Since hindsight no longer leads to foresight after a shift in context, a corresponding change in management style may be called for.

Complicated Contexts: The Domain of Experts

Complicated contexts, unlike simple ones, may contain multiple right answers, and though there is a clear relationship between cause and effect, not everyone can see it. This is the realm of "known unknowns." While leaders in a simple context must sense, categorize, and respond to a situation, those in a complicated context must sense, *analyze*, and respond. This approach is not easy and often requires expertise: A motorist may know that something is wrong with his car because the engine is knocking, but he has to take it to a mechanic to diagnose the problem.

Because the complicated context calls for investigating several options—many of which may be excellent—good practice, as opposed to best practice, is more appropriate. For example, the customary approach to engineering a new cell phone might emphasize feature A over feature B, but an alternative plan—emphasizing feature C—might be equally valuable.

Another example is the search for oil or mineral deposits. The effort usually requires a team of experts, more than one place will potentially produce results, and the location of the right spots for drilling or mining involves complicated analysis and understanding of consequences at multiple levels.

Entrained thinking is a danger in complicated contexts, too, but it is the experts (rather than the leaders) who are prone to it, and they tend to dominate the domain. When this problem occurs, innovative suggestions by nonexperts may be overlooked or dismissed, resulting in lost opportunities. The experts have, after all, invested in building their knowledge, and they are unlikely to tolerate controversial ideas. If the context has shifted, however, the leader may need access to those maverick concepts. To get around this issue, a leader must listen to the experts while simultaneously welcoming novel thoughts and solutions from others. Executives at one shoe manufacturer did this by opening up the brainstorming process for new shoe styles to the entire company. As a result, a security guard submitted a design for a shoe that became one of their best sellers.

Another potential obstacle is "analysis paralysis," where a group of experts hits a stalemate, unable to agree on any answers because of each individual's entrained thinking—or ego.

Working in unfamiliar environments can help leaders and experts approach decision making more creatively. For instance, we put retail marketing professionals in several military research environments for two weeks. The settings were unfamiliar and challenging, but they shared a primary similarity with the retail environment: In both cases, the marketers had to work with large volumes of data from which it was critical to identify small trends or weak signals. They discovered that there was little difference between, say, handling outgoing disaffected customers and anticipating incoming ballistic missiles. The exercise helped the marketing group learn how to detect a potential loss of loyalty and take action before a valued customer switched to a competitor. By improving their strategy, the marketers were able to retain far more high-volume business.

Games, too, can encourage novel thinking. We created a game played on a fictional planet that was based on the culture of a real client organization. When the executives "landed" on the alien planet, they were asked to address problems and opportunities facing the inhabitants. The issues they encountered were disguised but designed to mirror real situations, many of which were controversial or sensitive. Because the environment seemed so foreign and remote, however, the players found it much easier to come up with fresh ideas than they otherwise might have done. Playing a metaphorical game increases managers' willingness to experiment, allows them to resolve issues or problems more easily and creatively, and broadens the range of options in their decision-making processes. The goal of such games is to get as many perspectives as possible to promote unfettered analysis.

Reaching decisions in the complicated domain can often take a lot of time, and there is always a trade-off between finding the right answer and simply making a decision. When the right answer is elusive, however, and you must base your decision on incomplete data, your situation is probably complex rather than complicated.

Complex Contexts: The Domain of Emergence

In a complicated context, at least one right answer exists. In a complex context, however, right answers can't be ferreted out. It's like the difference between, say, a Ferrari and the Brazilian rainforest. Ferraris are com-plicated machines, but an expert mechanic can take one apart and reassemble it without changing a thing. The car is static, and the whole is the sum of its parts. The rainforest, on the other hand, is in constant flux—a species becomes extinct, weather patterns change, an agricultural project reroutes a water source—and the whole is far more than the sum of its parts. This is the realm of "unknown unknowns," and it is the domain to which much of contemporary business has shifted.

Most situations and decisions in organizations are complex because some major change—a bad quarter, a shift in management, a merger or acquisition—introduces unpredictability and flux. In this domain, we can under-stand why things happen only in retrospect. Instructive patterns, however, can emerge if the leader conducts experiments that are safe to fail. That is why, instead of attempting to impose a course of action, leaders must patiently allow the path forward to reveal itself. They need to probe first, then sense, and then respond.

There is a scene in the film *Apollo 13* when the astro-nauts encounter a crisis ("Houston, we have a problem") that moves the situation into a complex domain. A group of experts is put in a room with a mishmash of materials—bits of plastic and odds and ends that mirror the resources available to the astronauts in flight. Lead-ers tell the team: This is what you have; find a solution or the astronauts will die. None of those experts knew a pri-ori what would work. Instead, they had to let a solution emerge from the materials at hand. And they succeeded. (Conditions of scarcity often produce more creative results than conditions of abundance.)

Another example comes from YouTube. The founders could not possibly have predicted all the applications for streaming video technology that now exist. Once people started using YouTube creatively, however, the company could support and augment the emerging patterns of use. YouTube has become a popular platform for expressing political views, for example. The company built on this pattern by sponsoring a debate for presidential hopefuls with video feeds from the site.

As in the other contexts, leaders face several challenges in the complex domain. Of primary concern is the temptation to fall back into traditional command-and-control management styles—to demand fail-safe business plans with defined outcomes. Leaders who don't recognize that a complex domain requires a more experimental mode of management may become impatient when they don't seem to be achieving the results they were aiming for. They may also find it difficult to tolerate failure, which is an essential aspect of experimental understanding. If they try to overcontrol the organization, they will preempt the opportunity for informative patterns to emerge. Leaders who try to impose order in a complex context will fail, but those who set the stage, step back a bit, allow patterns to emerge, and determine which ones are desirable will succeed. (See the insert "Tools for Managing in a Complex Context.") They will discern many opportunities for innovation, creativity, and new business models.

Chaotic Contexts: The Domain of Rapid Response

In a chaotic context, searching for right answers would be pointless: The relationships between cause and effect are impossible to determine because they shift constantly and no manageable patterns exist—only turbulence. This is the realm of unknowables. The events of September 11, 2001, fall into this category.

In the chaotic domain, a leader's immediate job is not to discover patterns but to stanch the bleeding. A leader must first *act* to establish order, then sense where stability is present and from where it is absent, and then respond by working to transform the situation from chaos to complexity, where the identification of emerging patterns can both help prevent future crises and discern new opportunities. Communication of the most direct top-down or broadcast kind is imperative; there's simply no time to ask for input.

Unfortunately, most leadership "recipes" arise from examples of good crisis management. This is a mistake, and not only because chaotic situations are mercifully rare. Though the events of September 11 were not immediately comprehensible, the crisis demanded decisive action. New York's mayor at the time, Rudy Giuliani, demonstrated exceptional effectiveness under chaotic conditions by issuing directives and taking action to reestablish order. However, in his role as mayor—certainly one of the most complex jobs in the world—he was widely criticized for the same top-down leadership style that proved so enormously effective during the catastrophe. He was also criticized afterward for suggesting that elections be postponed so he could maintain order and stability. Indeed, a specific danger for leaders following a crisis is that some of them become less successful when the context shifts because they are not able to switch styles to match it.

Moreover, leaders who are highly successful in chaotic contexts can develop an overinflated self-image, becoming legends in their own minds. When they generate cultlike adoration, leading actually becomes harder for them because a circle of admiring supporters cuts them off from accurate information.

Yet the chaotic domain is nearly always the best place for leaders to impel innovation. People are more open to novelty and directive leadership in these situations than they would be in other contexts. One excellent technique is to manage chaos and innovation in parallel: The minute you encounter a crisis, appoint a reliable manager or crisis management team to resolve the issue. At the same time, pick out a separate team and focus its members on the opportunities for doing things differently. If you wait until the crisis is over, the chance will be gone.

Leadership Across Contexts

Good leadership requires openness to change on an individual level. Truly adept leaders will know not only how to identify the context they're working in at any given time but also how to change their behavior and their decisions to match that context. They also prepare their organization to understand the different contexts and the conditions for transition between them. Many leaders lead effectively—though usually in only one or two domains (not in all of them) and few, if any, prepare their organizations for diverse contexts.

During the Palatine murders of 1993, Deputy Chief Gasior faced four contexts at once. He had to take immediate action via the media to stem the tide of initial panic by keeping the community informed (chaotic); he had to help keep the department running routinely and according to established procedure (simple); he had to call in experts (complicated); and he had to continue to calm the community in the days and weeks following the crime (complex). That last situation proved the most challenging. Parents were afraid to let their children go to school, and employees were concerned about safety in their workplaces. Had Gasior misread the context as simple, he might just have said, "Carry on," which would have done nothing to reassure the community. Had he misread it as complicated, he might have called in experts to say it was safe—risking a loss of credibility and trust. Instead, Gasior set up a forum for business owners, high school students, teachers, and parents to share concerns and hear the facts. It was the right approach for a complex context: He allowed solutions to emerge from the community itself rather than trying to impose them.

BUSINESS SCHOOLS AND ORGANIZATIONS equip leaders to operate in ordered domains (simple and complicated), but most leaders usually must rely on their natural capabilities when operating in unordered contexts (complex and chaotic). In the face of greater complexity today, however, intuition, intellect, and charisma are no longer enough. Leaders need tools and approaches to guide their firms through less familiar waters.

In the complex environment of the current business world, leaders often will be called upon to act against their instincts. They will need to know when to share power and when to wield it alone, when to look to the wisdom of the group and when to take their own counsel. A deep understanding of context, the ability to embrace complexity and paradox, and a willingness to flexibly change leadership style will be required for leaders who want to make things happen in a time of increasing uncertainty.

Decisions in Multiple Contexts: A Leader's Guide

Effective leaders learn to shift their decision-making styles to match changing business environments. Simple, complicated, complex, and chaotic contexts each call for different managerial responses. By correctly identifying the governing context, staying aware of danger signals, and avoiding inappropriate reactions, managers can lead effectively in a variety of situations.

	The Context's Characteristics	The Leader's Job	Danger Signals	Response to Danger Signals
SIMPLE	Repeating patterns and consistent events Clear cause-and-effect relationships evident to everyone; right answer exists Known knowns Fact-based management	Sense, categorize, respond Ensure that proper processes are in place Delegate Use best practices Communicate in clear, direct ways Understand that extensive interactive communication may not be necessary	Complacency and comfort Desire to make complex problems simple Entrained thinking No challenge of received wisdom Overreliance on best practice if context shifts	Create communication channels to challenge orthodoxy Stay connected without micromanaging Don't assume things are simple Recognize both the value and the limitations of best practice
COMPLI-CATED	Expert diagnosis required Cause-and-effect relationships discoverable but not immediately apparent to everyone; more than one right answer possible Known unknowns Fact-based management	Sense, analyze, respond Create panels of experts Listen to conflicting advice	Experts overconfident in their own solutions or in the efficacy of past solutions Analysis paralysis Expert panels Viewpoints of nonexperts excluded	Encourage external and internal stakeholders to challenge expert opinions to combat entrained thinking Use experiments and games to force people to think outside the familiar

	Context characteristics	The leader's job	Danger signals	Response to danger signals
COMPLEX	Flux and unpredictability No right answers; emergent instructive patterns Unknown unknowns Many competing ideas A need for creative and innovative approaches Pattern-based leadership	Probe, sense, respond Create environments and experiments that allow patterns to emerge Increase levels of interaction and communication Use methods that can help generate ideas: Open up discussion (as through large group methods); set barriers; stimulate attractors; encourage dissent and diversity; and manage starting conditions and monitor for emergence	Temptation to fall back into habitual, command-and-control mode Temptation to look for facts rather than allowing patterns to emerge Desire for accelerated resolution of problems or exploitation of opportunities	Be patient and allow time for reflection Use approaches that encourage interaction so patterns can emerge
CHAOTIC	High turbulence No clear cause-and-effect relationships, so no point in looking for right answers Unknowables Many decisions to make and no time to think High tension Pattern-based leadership	Act, sense, respond Look for what works instead of seeking right answers Take immediate action to reestablish order (command and control) Provide clear, direct communication	Applying a command-and-control approach longer than needed "Cult of the leader" Missed opportunity for innovation Chaos unabated	Set up mechanisms (such as parallel teams) to take advantage of opportunities afforded by a chaotic environment Encourage advisers to challenge your point of view once the crisis has abated Work to shift the context from chaotic to complex

Understanding Complexity

COMPLEXITY IS MORE A WAY of thinking about the world than a new way of working with mathematical models. Over a century ago, Frederick Winslow Taylor, the father of scientific management, revolutionized leadership. Today, advances in complexity science, combined with knowledge from the cognitive sciences, are transforming the field once again. Complexity is poised to help current and future leaders make sense of advanced technology, globalization, intricate markets, cultural change, and much more. In short, the science of complexity can help all of us address the challenges and opportunities we face in a new epoch of human history.

A complex system has the following characteristics:

- It involves large numbers of interacting elements.
- The interactions are nonlinear, and minor changes can produce disproportionately major consequences.
- The system is dynamic, the whole is greater than the sum of its parts, and solutions can't be imposed; rather, they arise from the circumstances. This is frequently referred to as *emergence*.
- The system has a history, and the past is integrated with the present; the elements evolve with one another and with the environment; and evolution is irreversible.
- Though a complex system may, in retrospect, appear to be ordered and predictable, hindsight

does not lead to foresight because the external conditions and systems constantly change.

- Unlike in ordered systems (where the system constrains the agents), or chaotic systems (where there are no constraints), in a complex system the agents and the system constrain one another, especially over time. This means that we cannot forecast or predict what will happen.

One of the early theories of complexity is that complex phenomena arise from simple rules. Consider the rules for the flocking behavior of birds: Fly to the center of the flock, match speed, and avoid collision. This simple-rule theory was applied to industrial modeling and production early on, and it promised much; but it did not deliver in isolation. More recently, some thinkers and practitioners have started to argue that human complex systems are very different from those in nature and cannot be modeled in the same ways because of human unpredictability and intellect. Consider the following ways in which humans are distinct from other animals:

- They have multiple identities and can fluidly switch between them without conscious thought. (For example, a person can be a respected member of the community as well as a terrorist.)
- They make decisions based on past patterns of success and failure, rather than on logical, definable rules.
- They can, in certain circumstances, purposefully change the systems in which they operate to equilibrium states (think of a Six Sigma project) in order to create predictable outcomes.

Leaders who want to apply the principles of complexity science to their organizations will need to think and act differently than they have in the past. This may not be easy, but it is essential in complex contexts.

Tools for Managing in a Complex Context

GIVEN THE AMBIGUITIES of the complex domain, how can leaders lead effectively?

- **Open up the discussion.** Complex contexts require more interactive communication than any of the other domains. Large group methods (LGMs), for instance, are efficient approaches to initiating democratic, interactive, multidirectional discussion sessions. Here, people generate innovative ideas that help leaders with development and execution of complex decisions and strategies. For example, "positive deviance" is a type of LGM that allows people to discuss solutions that are already working within the organization itself, rather than looking to outside best practices for clues about how to proceed. The Plexus Institute used this approach to address the complex problem of hospital-acquired infections, resulting in behavior change that lowered the incidence by as much as 50%.

- **Set barriers.** Barriers limit or delineate behavior. Once the barriers are set, the system can self-regulate within those boundaries. The founders of eBay, for example, created barriers by establishing a simple set of rules. Among them are pay on time, deliver merchandise quickly, and provide full disclosure on the condition of the merchandise. Participants police themselves by rating one another on the quality of their behavior.

- **Stimulate attractors.** Attractors are phenomena that arise when small stimuli and probes (whether from leaders or others) resonate with people. As attractors gain momentum, they provide structure and coherence. EBay again provides an illustrative example. In 1995, founder Pierre Omidyar launched an offering called Auction Web on his personal website. His probe, the first item for sale, quickly morphed into eBay, a remarkable attractor for people who want to buy and sell things. Today, sellers on eBay continue to provide experimental probes that create attractors of various types. One such probe, selling a car on the site, resonated with buyers, and soon automobile sales became a popular attractor.

- **Encourage dissent and diversity.** Dissent and formal debate are valuable communication assets in complex contexts because they encourage the emergence of well-forged patterns and ideas. A "ritual dissent" approach, for instance, puts parallel teams to work on the same problem in a large group meeting environment. Each team appoints a spokesperson who moves from that team's table to another team's table. The spokesperson presents the first group's conclusions while the second group listens in silence. The spokesperson then turns around to face away from the second team, which rips into the presentation, no holds barred, while the spokesperson listens quietly. Each team's spokesperson visits other tables in turn; by the end of the session, all the ideas have been well dissected and honed. Taking turns listening in silence helps everyone understand the value of listening carefully, speaking openly, and not taking criticism personally.

- **Manage starting conditions and monitor for emergence.** Because outcomes are unpredictable in a complex context, leaders need to focus on creating an environment from which good things can emerge, rather than trying to bring about predetermined results and possibly missing opportunities that arise unexpectedly. Many years ago, for instance, 3M instituted a rule allowing its researchers to spend 15% of their time on any project that interested them. One result was a runaway success: the Post-it Note.

Originally published in November 2007
Reprint R0711C

About the Contributors

MARTHA AMRAM is an author, speaker, and consultant, and at the time her article was written was president of Glaze Creek Partners in Palo Alto, California.

MARY E. BOONE is the president of Boone Associates, a consulting firm in Essex, Connecticut.

KEVIN BUEHLER is a director at McKinsey and is based in New York.

HUGH COURTNEY is Director and Chairman of the Board at D&E Communications, Incorporated.

JOHN DRZIK is the president and CEO of New York–based Mercer Oliver Wyman, a global financial services consulting firm.

ANDREW FREEMAN is a senior expert on risk at McKinsey and is based in London.

KENNETH A. FROOT is a professor at the Harvard Business School in Boston, Massachusetts.

JOSEPH FULLER is the CEO of Monitor Group, a global professional services firm headquartered in Cambridge, Massachusetts.

RON HULME is a director at McKinsey and is based in Houston.

JANE KIRKLAND is Managing Director of her own consulting firm, Kirkland Partners, and also teaches custom executive education programs at Dartmouth's Tuck School.

NALIN KULATILAKA is Wing Tat Lee Family Professor of Management and a Professor of Finance at the Boston University School of Management.

PAUL SAFFO is a forecaster based in Silicon Valley, in California.

DAVID S. SCHARFSTEIN is Edmund Cogswell Converse Professor of Finance and Banking at the Harvard Business School in Boston, Massachusetts.

DAVID J. SNOWDON is the founder and chief scientific officer of Competitive Edge, an international research network.

ADRIAN J. SLYWOTZKY is a Boston-based managing director of Mercer Management Consulting and a coauthor of *How to Grow When Markets Don't* (Warner Business Books, 2003).

JEREMY C. STEIN is the Moise Y. Safra Professor of Economics at Harvard University.

PATRICK VIGUERIE is a director at McKinsey.

Index

traditional approaches and, 153–155

Stulz, René, 6

subprime default rates, 12–13

Suncor, 21

Sun Microsystems, 8

swaps, 13, 94

"synthetic CDOs," 8

Target, 50, 58

Taylor, Frederick Winslow, 200

technological innovation, and risk, 7–9, 46–48, 159

terminal value, 113

Texas Instruments, 7

3M company, 204

Time Warner, 145

timing, and risk, 60, 137

timing options, 103

Tosco, 21

Toyota, and Prius development, 54–55

The Toyota Way (Liker), 55

trigger events, 164, 173

true ambiguity, 159–160
analytic tools in, 162, 165
strategy in, 178–180
as transitory, 159, 160, 180

True Value Hardware, 45

Tsutaya, 53

UBS, 20

uncertainty. *See* forecasting

underinvestment problem, 6

unfamiliar work environments, 191–192

U. S. Defense Advanced Research Projects Agency (DARPA), 186

Universal, 45–46

unknowables. *See* complex contexts

"unknown knowns." *See* complex contexts

UPS, 171

Valero, 21

valuation. *See also* real-options approach
of equity versus debt, 73
flaws in traditional approach to, 113, 114–115, 119–120
level 2 uncertainty and, 163
level 3 uncertainty and, 164

values, and risk management, 18

Visa, 45, 49

VisiCalc (spreadsheet), 7

Wall Street. *See also* market discipline

executive compensation and, 33–35

strategic decision making and, 26–27, 29–31

Wal-Mart, 50, 58

wild cards, and forecasting, 133–135

workforce
 executive commitment to
  business and, 35–36
 simple decision making and,
  189–190
WorldCom, 32

Y2K, as wild card, 134
"You Have More Capital Than
  You Think" (HBR November
  2005), 9
YouTube, 193–194